CW00743301

PAULINA DLAMINI
Servant of two kings

Killie Campbell Africana Library Publications

Number 1.   PAULINA DLAMINI: SERVANT OF TWO KINGS
            Compiled by H. Filter; edited and translated by S. Bourquin

Zululand and Natal showing places mentioned
in the text. Natal boundaries as in 1879.

PAULINA DLAMINI
Servant of two kings

Compiled by

H. FILTER

Edited and translated by

S. BOURQUIN

Killie Campbell Africana Library
Durban
and
University of Natal Press
Pietermaritzburg
1986

© University of Natal 1986
Box 375, Pietermaritzburg, 3200 South Africa

ISBN 0 86980 523 1
ISBN 0 86980 529 0 (Set)

Typeset in the University of Natal Press
Pietermaritzburg
Printed by Kohler Carton and Print
Box 955, Pinetown, 3600 South Africa

Contents

Illustrations

Editor's Preface

As a lad of nine or ten years I spent many hours sitting on a box in my father's study on a remote mission station in Hlubiland, avidly reading and rereading stories in Longman's *Primers* and *Readers*, which were stored there for periodic distribution to the small mission schools, scattered throughout the foothills of the southern Drakensberg. This was part of my early education because, until the age of eleven, I did not attend any formal school, but was taught by my parents everything that they thought I ought to know. One of the stories I remember clearly to this day — its title was *Ulundi*. It aroused my enduring interest in the history of the Zulu.

The Maritzburg College library provided additional reading during my subsequent school years and to this I added over a further period of some fifty years. But I have never succeeded in filling all the gaps, clarifying obscurities or finding all the answers to even apparently simple questions. However, through some good fortune, this slender volume contains at least some answers and even some intimate detail concerning the every day life at the royal *umuzi* of *Ondini* and its illustrious occupant, King Cetshwayo.

I am grateful that there was a person with so lucid a memory as Nomguqo Dlamini and a man with the perspicacity and care of Heinrich Filter to record her recollections. It was with considerable alacrity that I responded to the challenge of getting these memoirs published in a way which would make them accessible not only to white readers, but particularly also to the Zulu people. My only regret is that very many more of her recollections were not recorded and preserved for posterity.

Apart from the facts surrounding Cetshwayo's person there are sidelights on other personalities, such as Masiphula and Mbilini. Zibhebhu's covetousness, for instance, makes sad reading when one considers the prestige he gained and the loyalty he showed during the Anglo-Zulu war itself.

The existing volume of recorded traditional Zulu poetry is relatively small, mainly due perhaps to the fact that it employs much metaphorical language and obscure allusions which become intelligible only if read in context with the description of some event or happening. The songs remembered by Paulina and contained herein will, hopefully, add fresh material to what is already known.

The insight which Paulina gives, through personal experience, into the battle which is being waged for freedom from superstition and from spiritual bondage on the one hand, and against the evil 'earth spirits', the *amandiki* and *amandawe*, and the *fufunyana* syndrome, on the other, are, additionally, of special interest.

Lastly, as there is a growing interest among many Zulu in the genealogy of individuals and families, most of the names remembered by Paulina, even of ordinary, homely folk, have been included. They might assist some Zulu families in tracing their forebears and add to the fullness of understanding of the Zulu past.

A sincere word of thanks is due to Ms M. P. Moberly of the University of Natal Press for the assistance and advice received in preparing these papers for publication; and also to Ms J. Shier who compiled the index.

S. BOURQUIN

Introduction

The reminiscences recorded in these papers are those of a Zulu woman, gifted with an excellent memory, who began her adolescent life as a member of King Cetshwayo's household. Paulina's recollections are of more than passing interest because here, for the first time as far as I can establish, a glimpse is given of the intimate, everyday domestic life of the royal establishment, at a period when western influences had not as yet intruded into the traditional life of the Zulu people. Much has been written about Cetshwayo and his time as a result of his involvement in an armed conflict with Great Britain, the mightiest empire of that time. But Paulina, Nomguqo as she was then known, was a Zulu girl still in her teens. She was not concerned with matters of state, politics and international relations — these were, in any case, matters left for the attention of men. She, as a woman, tells about the things which were of concern to the inhabitants of the royal establishment, the chores of daily life, the benefits, the punishments, and in the centre of it all the habits of the man who was the heir apparent to the Zulu throne and who eventually did become king. With childlike simplicity she states that she liked the king and he liked her, even though she was merely a servant without any personal involvement. She obviously enjoyed her status and her life as a member of the king's household. But, in retrospect, she also expresses concern at some aspects of the Zulu traditional life, the power over life and death which the king wielded and the belief in magic and superstition; of these her subsequent conversion to Christianity made her highly critical.

Her reminiscences might have become lost to the world had it not been for the interest shown in her story by a missionary colleague and his appreciation that what she had to tell was unique in many respects. It was the Reverend Heinrich Filter, a minister of the Hermannsburg Mission Society, who recorded the information on which this narrative is based. Heinrich Filter was born on 6 June 1893 at Etombe in the Piet Retief district. His father, son of one of the early missionaries, was farming near Lüneburg when the Anglo-Boer War of 1899-1902 broke out. At that time Lüneburg was part of the South African Republic and, as Transvalers, the family was lodged in a British concentration camp at Volksrust. After the war young Heinrich attended a farm school; but outside of school hours he had to help his father re-establish the devastated farm.

A growing urge to become a missionary, as his grandfather had been, prompted the eighteen-year old Heinrich to leave home in 1912 and to enter the mission seminary at Hermannsburg in Germany. However, his studies were interrupted when the First World War broke out and, as a South African and British subject, he was interned at Spandau. After a captivity of close on two years he was released on parole for the purpose of working in Clausthal hospital as a nurse. This hospital training and experience proved invaluable in his subsequent missionary career.

After the war he resumed his studies and passed his final theological examinations in 1923, whereupon he married and returned with his bride to Natal. He received his first posting to Lemgo, a mission station in the Emakhosini region of Zululand. At the end of 1926, having lost his wife in childbirth, Revd Filter re-married and spent the following three years at the newly founded station Esibongweni (the place of thanksgiving), the ancestral home of the Buthelezi clan. This station was not very far from Lemgo. During the years to come he served at a number of other mission establishments and also became a member of a committee composed of representatives of various Lutheran mission societies engaged in the translation of the Bible into Zulu. He retired in 1963 and died six years later on 31 August 1969.

When Filter took up his first posting at Lemgo he met Paulina Nomguqo Dlamini serving as an evangelist and found her not only a dedicated member of his congregation, but also a person whose support, guidance and advice were of inestimable value to the young missionary. She was the driving force behind the Christianisation of so many of her people, that she was occasionally alluded to as the 'Apostle' of Northern Zululand. She is given credit for the establishment of a number of mission stations in that region. Even after his transfer to Esibongweni he maintained close contact with her.

It may be presumed that very early in their association Revd Filter must have realised the uniqueness of Paulina's reminiscences and the importance of preserving as much of this information as he could, for he began to keep notes of his discussions with her about her background and young life. These discussions appear to have commenced about the year 1925, when, it seems, Paulina was about sixty-seven years old. They were spread over a number of years, with breaks of several years. The notes made at those discussions consist of handwritten records of Paulina's dictations in Zulu, subsequently transcribed in type.

Realising that Paulina was getting on in years and that much of her valuable information ought to be recorded, Revd Filter renewed his efforts early in 1939 by bringing her from Lemgo to his own station Nazareth, near Elandskraal, where she became a guest in the Filter home. According to Mrs Anna Filter, her husband would engage Paulina in leisurely discussions about the past whenever an opportunity offered itself during the day or in the early evenings, recording in manuscript any items of interest or concern. As these discussions were conducted intermittently and covered a variety of subjects and reminiscences, they were written on loose sheets of paper without sequence or cohesion. Revd Filter then collected these notes under specific headings and rewrote them in the form of a coherent narrative, aiming at a chronologically correct sequence. It seems probable that some of these notes, having been transcribed were not properly filed and were lost.

In the opening chapter Revd Filter has cast the basic

information obtained from Paulina in a literary form, involving, for instance Paulina's father Sikhunyana Dlamini in a dialogue with Maboya Buthelezi. Even though the rest of the story is also a narrative, and not a verbatim record, he has adhered as closely as possible to the original record. It must be borne in mind, however, that these statements were jotted down in long-hand, in the form of key words or brief sentences. In gathering them together and rearranging them into a narrative, Revd Filter expanded them into full and consecutive sentences.

In introducing herself and relating the story of her birth, Paulina merely records brief and basic facts which she had heard from her father. In order to create an atmosphere and to give some form and colour to the bare skeleton provided by Paulina's statements, Revd Filter indulged in a small amount of padding. This becomes obvious when he involves some of the characters in direct speech; but this literary licence is restricted to the opening pages of this book and does not impair the genuineness of Paulina's reminiscences as such.

There are also other instances of editorial interference; for example, that Mr Theophilus Shepstone was accompanied, inter alia, by a military band, when he attended Cetshwayo's coronation. The European type of music, bands and musical instruments, except drums, were unknown to the Zulu, and their language contained no words to desctibe them. Paulina's only reference to this band consists therefore of the two terse words '*kwezwakala isigubu*' (literally it being heard drum). For the sake of presenting a picture that is full and unquestionably correct — and at the same time entertaining — this has been rendered, by both author and editor in their respective languages as 'there was military music and a crashing of drums' (p. 31). Both have taken care, however, that any liberty of expression has not introduced fiction or a distortion of Paulina's own basic memories.

Revd Filter had prepared this narrative in German for publication as a mission brochure and had also included some matters which were of purely missionary interest, but irrelevant to Paulina's story. His death brought this project to a halt, until his widow, Mrs Anna Filter, made all the material available to me. I considered much of the contents so unique and of such great interest as to deserve much wider publicity than originally intented; hence my undertaking to translate the story into English and, at the same time, to revise and edit it.

In the course of translation from German into English great care was taken to adhere as closely as practicable to the original Zulu idiom. This care was necessary because, while bound to follow Revd Filter's narrative, it was important that the involvement of a third language did not result in any material deviation in meaning from Paulina's own Zulu modes of expression. For instance, the German version (G.100, File 5) contains the sentence: '*Majestät, der Du königlichen Geschlechts bist, wir danken Dir*'. A straight translation into English would result in the statement: 'Majesty, you who are of royal blood, we thank thee'. However, Paulina's statement (Z.52, File 6) reads: '*Ndabezitha, wena wohlanga, siyakubonga*' which in English, has been rendered herein – more correctly I believe – as, '*Ndabezitha*, Lord of the Nation, we thank thee!' The word *uhlanga* is of deep mythical significance as it refers not so much to 'royal blood' as to the original stem or stock from which Unkulunkulu (the 'Great Progenitor') emerged, bringing with him mankind and nationhood.

Ndabezitha is a Zulu title and is composed of *indaba* + *izitha* which literally means 'matter discussed by the enemy'. It is a metaphor used as a mark of great respect in addressing the king, a chief or some other exalted person. In the German version it appears as '*Majestät*' (majesty) but no attempt has been made here to translate it into English. This and several other words are so specifically Zulu, that no translation can really do justice to their inherent meaning. They have been retained in their Zulu form, but their specific meaning has been explained in the list of annotations. Other examples are, for instance:

> *isiGodlo* – The German version uses the word *Klausur* of which the English translation would be 'confinement, seclusion, enclosure, cloister'. As neither language can

provide an acceptable translation, the Zulu word has been retained in the text.

inDuna —   The German version uses the word *Minister* throughout; but in Zulu this title could denote, depending on the context, a head-man, official, councillor, or senior officer in the Zulu army (see Note 15).

When I undertook this project I discussed with Mrs Filter what should become of the documents once I had completed my work and she readily agreed that they should be lodged in the Killie Campbell Africana Library where they are available to researchers. But the interest of this story is not confined to researchers and this publication is intended to make Paulina's reminiscences accessible to a wide range of readers and to fill in some of the detail that until now has been missing from the tapestry depicting one of the most interesting periods in Natal and Zulu history.

Details of the Filter records

The numbers in the margins of the printed text refer to File 5 (German) and File 6 (Zulu) where the paragraphs have been numbered consecutively.

File 1   A collection of statements made by Paulina at different times, written in long-hand (pencil and ink), some pages in type. 36 pages numbered consecutively. In addition pages in red type, numbered 1–8, followed by handwritten pages in ink, numbered 9b–34b. Some papers are tattered; the file appears to be incomplete.

File 2   Heading on first page in German 'Lebensbeschreibung von Paulina Dlamini nach dem Diktat am 7 März 25', followed by a typed Zulu text and further statements in Zulu dated 7/10/1928, 11/10/1928, etc. Pages numbered 1–62. Most of the typed material consists of transcripts from File 1, but there are also some aspects for which there are no corresponding manuscript notes in File 1.

File 3   Marked 'Paulina in Zulu, Kopie Nr. 1'. Typescript draft of Paulina's story in Zulu, based on information and text contained in File 2, but re-arranged, for instance, information from p.23 of File 2 now appears on p.1 of File 3. Corrections in red ink. Pages 1—70. In addition pages 52—58 in Zulu, typescript corrected with red and blue ink, dealing with evangelisation and other missionary matters.

File 4   Loose foolscap sheets of a pencilled draft translation of the Zulu version into German, pages 1—17; also loose sheets of a draft translation of the Zulu version in ink, pages 1—35; also what seems to be the first draft of the German translation in typescript, pages 1—82.

File 5   Paulina's story in German, typescript, complete, pages 1—112, except page 55 which is missing. My impression is that this is due to a typographical error in numbering the pages, and not to a page as such having been lost. All the paragraphs have been numbered consecutively in the margin.

File 6   Editor's photostat working copy of Paulina's story in Zulu, same as Files 2 and 3. The Zulu text from File 3 has consecutive paragraph numbers in the margin.

Envelope containing 28 letters or copies of letters dealing with the Zulu allegation that the remains of Piet Retief and his followers were buried in a donga, 1942—1956. See Note 8.

Compiler's Preface

Many friends have asked me repeatedly to write comprehensively about Paulina, the 'Apostle of Northern Zululand'. Lack of time has prevented me until now from doing so; but now that I have retired, I will endeavour to sketch Paulina's remarkable life. In doing so I do not wish to glorify Paulina, for the glory belongs to God, who has used this Zulu woman to exemplify the promise made by Our Lord Jesus Christ that: 'If anyone is thirsty let him come to me; whoever believes in me, let him drink.' As the Scriptures say: 'Streams of living water shall flow out from within him.' John 7, 38.

Who was Paulina? On her father's side she was related to the royal house of the Swazis. On her mother's side she counted the freebooter and famous founder of the Matabele kingdom, Mzilikazi, as a great-uncle.

Her father gave her the meaningful name Unomguqo (the Kneeling One). At first she had to kneel before the earthly king of the Zulus, Cetshwayo, in order to recognize the splendour of the Zulu empire as a vain and transitory realm of this world. However, when, in a vision, she had been filled with the glory of the realm of God, she fell to her knees before the King of Kings, Jesus Christ, and followed His call to become the apostle of northern Zululand.

I was granted the privilege to work with her for six years at Lemgo and Esibongweni mission stations. I learnt much from her and often sought her advice and counsel. That which she told me about her life and which I recorded, I now wish to present in a comprehensive and readable form, as a testimony to her dedication and as an encouragement to others to further the missionwork among the Zulus. May God bless this endeavour.

HEINRICH FILTER
1967

Paulina Dlamini *Servant of two kings*

INTRODUCTION

Z.1,2
G.1   Baba Mhlahlela,[1] you wish to hear my life's story so
that you may reduce it to writing. Yes, indeed, there is
much I can tell you, as to how I grew up and as to how I
served my king, Cetshwayo, as a member of his *isigodlo*.[2] I
liked him as he liked me. We respected him greatly for he
had tremendous prestige. I saw him at the height of his
kingly authority; but I also saw him at the end of his reign,
which was destroyed at the hands of the British government.

But what fills me with utter amazement to this very day
is the manner of my conversion to the service of my Lord
Jesus Christ which I experienced while I was a member of
the household of Shede Foloyi [Gert van Rooyen][3] at
Hlimbithwa near Mgungundlovana [Greytown] in Natal.
However, I do not wish to commence my tale with my
conversion and how God used me as his instrument to
kindle and then to rouse the flame of faith here in northern
Zululand. Rather let me first relate details of my life as a
pagan member of the Zulu royal establishment, in order
that my subsequent conversion may bear so much stronger
testimony to the wondrous grace of God which he granted
me and manifested through me. But I must first tell you
about my parents and my childhood.

1 Servant of Cetshwayo

MY PARENTAL HOME

Z.3,5,13
G.2

Not far from where the town of Vryheid stands today, in a fertile region on the upper reaches of the Mkhuze River, stood the large *umuzi*[4] of Maboya kaMbundulwane Buthelezi.[5] This fertile region had previously been occupied by the Zulu general and subsequent freebooter, Mzilikazi, and his people. Maboya Buthelezi had then requested King Dingane for an allocation of this area to himself and his clan, on account of the excellence of the grazing. Maboya was a rich and prominent man who had served Dingane as a warrior for many a year, and had previously had his *umuzi* near where the mission station Esibongweni stands today.

Z.4
G.3

Not only was Maboya rich in cattle and had many wives, but he also held in bondage a member of the royal house of the Swazi. On one of Dingane's campaigns against the Swazi, Maboya Buthelezi had captured a boy and the cattle he was herding at King Sobhuza's[6] Nobamba kraal. The captive, Prince Sikhunyane Dlamini Nkosi, son of Majingwa, son of Sobhuza, king of the Swazis, became Maboya's bondsman and grew up at Maboya's kraal, kwaMandeva, where the Esibongweni mission station stands today. He was my father. He became a prominent man, boasting five wives and a large herd of cattle.

Z.10
G.4

He came into prominence and built up his fortune under King Mpande,[7] when he became the king's messenger. As a born Swazi he was intelligent and fleet of foot. It was one of his tasks to collect the cattle which the Zulus had to surrender to their king by way of a tribute. Mpande rewarded him richly for these services. He also had to accompany the king's *induna*, Umundula Nxumalo, at all times.

Z.5
G.5

On many a cold evening around the fire father would tell us about his earlier years. Mingled with the sadness of

his capture and the loss of family and home was the joy
and satisfaction of his present state and his service to such
great Zulu kings as Dingane and Mpande. He took particular
pleasure in recounting the events of the day when Piet Retief
and his companions were killed, and rejoiced in the fact
that he knew where Piet Retief lay buried, a fact which
he claimed to be a secret, the revelation of which would be
punishable by death.[8]

Z.6
G.6-10
My father belonged to the iHlaba regiment,[9] which had
been raised by Dingane. It was this regiment, which was
charged with the task of killing Piet Retief and his men.
The king had not intended that they should be killed,
because they had come merely to ask, in a reasonable
manner, for land and grazing for their flocks. After the
king had already granted them land he was advised by the
great *induna*, Ndlela, the son of Sompisi of the Ntuli
clan,[10] who took all decisions on behalf of the king, that
Piet Retief and his followers should be killed. He persuaded
Dingane that Piet Retief deserved to be killed, because
he had really come only to oust Dingane from his land and
his possessions. Piet Retief and his companions should be
invited to join the king in the cattle kraal, but to leave
their weapons at the entrance. Piet Retief, when approached, accepted the invitation and the white men
actually entered the kraal unarmed. The warriors encircled,
then surrounded those inside. They then raised their voices
in a war song with the following words:

Yiya, yiya, yiya
Muntu wami kwaZulu!
Babezithela obisini.
Muntu wami kwaZulu,
Abafokazana babethi:
Kayikungena eNgome!
Wangena.
Nawe, Nhlanganiso,
Wawuphika inkani ukuthi
Kayikushisa uMhlahlandlela.
Awusekho! Awusekho!
Heyayé, heyayé!

Muntu wami kwaZulu,
Wangena!
Wakhuza IWAWA,
Wangena!

Go, go, go
My Zulu fellow!
They plunged into disaster.
My Zulu fellow,
Poor strangers said
He would not enter the Ngome forest!
Yet he entered.
You too, Nhlanganiso,[11]
You argued obstinately, saying
He will not burn Mhlahlandlela.[12]
He is no more, no longer in existence!
Bravo, bravo!
My Zulu fellow,
He entered!
He shouted the war-cry,
And then he entered!

At the word 'IWAWA' they followed with 'MBO' [strike]!
My father said, 'On that day our arms grew weary. We
struck the white men, we dragged them down. As we
struck them we shouted to one another: "You strike from
above!" or "You strike from below!" They died horrible
deaths in that kraal. They were not stabbed with spears,
they were beaten down with sticks. Only two white youths
escaped; the one was mounting a white horse.'

The bodies were first dragged to the spot where the
Piet Retief monument stands today. From there they were
dragged some two hundred paces in a north-easterly
direction and thrown in a heap into a donga.[13] The sides
of this donga were then collapsed to cover the bodies with
earth and stones.[14]

The bodies of the servants of the white men, who were
also killed, were left, however, close to where the monument
stands today. Thus Piet Retief's satchel was later found by
the Boers at this spot. My father also told us that he had
seen some shiny objects on the hands of some bodies.

Gert van Rooyen often questioned my father about these events, but he gave nothing away. He also forbade us to talk to others about them. You, Mhlahlela, must promise me, not to divulge this information during my lifetime; except that if you wish to write to people overseas about it you may do so.

I have seen the spot my father had described. We, Jeremia Buthelezi and I, later held church services at the place of Dazukile Sibiya, the *induna*[15] at Dingane's former kraal, Mgungundlovu. We asked Sibiya where Piet Retief was buried, but he would say nothing. On one of these occasions I secretly visited the spot my father had described and saw the depression in the ground.

Z.11
G.11-16

But I must now return to my own personal story.

I was deeply touched when my father told me about my birth and when he remembered the day on which, according to Zulu custom, he was restrained from entering the hut of his principal wife, my mother. With tender pride he remembered my mother, Nomhlwathi.[16] Her father, that is my grandfather, was Njiya Khumalo, a brother of Mzilikazi Khumalo, the same Mzilikazi who made a name for himself by breaking with Shaka and establishing his own great Matabele kingdom in the north.

On the day on which my father was debarred from entering my mother's hut, he had hoped that she would present him with a son. He watched as many women crawled into the hut from which only subdued voices could be heard. On that day Nomhlwathi was not at all well. As a precaution a medicine-man had been consulted. He had ordered that a magic remedy should be applied, if the child could not be delivered.

A woman emerged from the hut and approached Sikhunyane. 'How is it with Nomhlwathi?' he enquired and was told:

'The way is barred. The child cannot be delivered.'

'Have you applied the remedy?' he demanded to know.

'Master, I have come to ask whether this should be done.'

'Of course, immediately; you should not have waited so long.'

The old midwife removed herself to fetch a broken

earthenware vessel with glowing embers. Inside the hut the magic remedy, consisting of a variety of hair and other substances from wild animals, was thrown on the burning coals and the labouring woman enshrouded by its smoke. Then, suddenly, my father heard the women exclaim: 'The medicine has worked!'

When the old woman emerged again, he asked impatiently, 'How is it?'

'Dlamini Nkosi, it has found the way, it is alive.'

'Is it human?'

'Yes, it is a human being — not an animal.'

'What sort of being?'

'It is a girl.'

This, I am told, is how I was born.

My father would have preferred a boy as the first child from his favourite wife. But he was content with a daughter, believing that, as I had royal blood in my veins, I would one day add substantially to his herd of cattle.[17] But father never received any lobola cattle through me; as you know, I remained single and never married.

I was a tender and rather weak child, and, later on, I also suffered from asthma. Magic remedies were applied to shield me against witchcraft and all evil. So, for instance, I was taken to a hill where lightning had struck and given a herbal enema to protect me against the bird of the heavens, when lightning strikes.

Z.14;
G.17

I was given two names. My mother called me Khulumani [Speak Ye!] But more important was the name my father gave me. It was the rather significant name Unomguqo [the Kneeling One]. My father obviously did not realise the prophetic significance of this name. As his daughter I learnt, to start with, to bend my knees before the mighty Zulu king, Cetshwayo, but later on before the King of all Kings, Jesus Christ, whose foremost servant I was to become in the heart of Zululand.

Z.14;
G.18

I grew up much beloved by my parents. Unfortunately, my mother, whom I loved very much, died when I was still young. All the love my father had had for my mother he now bestowed on me, his favourite daughter. I was my mother's only daughter, neither did I have a brother through her. My father decreed, therefore, that my half-brother Umzondi, son of his wife from the Thusi clan, should be deemed to have been a son of my own mother, and thereby become my full brother. This made me very happy.

Z.11;
G.19-21 As I have already mentioned, my father had five wives. Firstly, he took to himself a girl from the Thusi clan. She bore him three sons, Umzondi, Unkonzo and Josiya, who was of the same age as Masimba Buthelezi, the guardian of the royal kraal, Nobamba. The second wife was a Mtshali girl from Bangisweni. She bore Umtiswazwe and two girls, Anna,[18] who married Sithole, and Uyinyongo. The third wife, born Mazibuko, had four children, two girls and two boys, Luka and Samuel. The last mentioned lives at Umnyathi. The girls were Lina and Nonkomosa. The fourth wife came from the Myeni family in the Lubombo mountains. Her father was Malinga Myeni. Her children are Hanna, Salome, Meliam [Miriam], Deborah and Andrease. The fifth wife was my mother. She belonged to the female regiment, Ugudludonga, which was raised in Mpande's times. At the time of the battle of Ndondakusuka she already wore an *isicholo*[19] ready to get married. As the only child of the principal wife I was addressed by all inhabitants of the *umuzi* as '*Inkosazana*'.[20]

When I had reached girlhood, my father's life and mine were affected by a sudden and unexpected turn of events. I wish to relate briefly how this came about.

One chilly day my father, Sikhunyane, sat sunning himself, with a blanket over his shoulders, minding his own thoughts. As it got a little warmer he was joined by the clan head, the greying Maboya Buthelezi, whom we held in great respect. His whole demeanour indicated that he was moved by weighty considerations and my father, who later told me about it, became quite anxious to hear what Buthelezi had to say.

Z.16;
G.22-35 They exchanged greetings and rejoiced at the first sunny morning after some chilly days; then Maboya became sparing of words, because apparently he did not quite know how to broach his subject. In order to achieve his purpose he steered the conversation towards the subject

of Cetshwayo, who in recent years had become much talked about. Cetshwayo and his actions provided sufficient substance to keep the daily gossip and even more serious discussions going. Skilfully he led the conversation towards a proposition which was to determine my whole future.

'Our king, Mpande, has grown old and weary and rightly has Cetshwayo taken the reins of government into his hands. He is beginning to show himself as a real leader of the people. The eyes of everybody are on him. Most people expect much of him and hope that he will revive the glory which marked the reign of his famous uncle Shaka. The younger generation yearns for glory through battle.'

My father replied: 'Rightly so. Our king has committed no great deeds. He is inactive and peaceloving. That is why we have peace; but our youth wants to see blood.'

Maboya interrupted him briskly: 'Yes, during the civil war our people have seen and smelt blood and are still intoxicated by it. This applies particularly to Cetshwayo's victorious Usuthu faction.'

'No doubt this war between brothers resulted from the jealousies and intrigues of certain royal wives,' commented my father. 'They all assailed the weak and indecisive Mpande with demands that he should nominate *their* sons as his successor. These women even agitated amongst the people for support of their individual claims, leading to the formation of the two mighty factions, the Izigqoza supporting prince Mbuyazwe and his followers, and the great Usuthu party backing Cetshwayo.'

The conversation became more animated as the two men remembered the day on which the royal succession was finally settled. Maboya smiled. 'Dlamini, do you remember the excitement and tension on that day when, in the presence of all his sons, the king suddenly declared, "Whoever can lift this vessel of beer shall succeed me as king!" '

'Yes,' replied my father, 'Cetshwayo did it. Last of all he powerfully strode up to the mighty *khamba*[21] of beer and looking around enquired softly: "How is it, my

brothers, that you cannot lift this vessel?" Then, bending
low, with one mighty swoop he lifted the *khamba* on
high. There was much applause. Filled with amazement
many put their hands to their mouths. Cetshwayo's
followers were jubilant, but Mbuyazwe's people felt
intensely vexed.'

Over an exchange of snuff the two men then relived the
day when the Usuthu and the Izigqoza met in battle at
Ndondakusuka, and when at the end of that day Cetshwayo
strode over the bodies of Mbuyazwe and five other brothers
and thousands of their fallen supporters, to emerge as the
undisputed successor to his father's throne. In fact, owing
to Mpande's incapacity Cetshwayo had become the regent,
and much talk revolved around his actions, his omissions
and his ways of governing.

In the meantime the sun had risen high. The *umuzi*
had already been swept clean. I, Nomguqo, had cleaned
my father's hut and had polished the floor. I had even
been away for some time to fetch a certain type of long
grass the stalks of which I had to set alight [as a candle]
and hold one after the other in the evenings. The cows
had already been milked and the women were busy preparing a meal.

When Maboya noticed that my father had fallen silent,
after indicating that he did not share entirely Maboya's
enthusiasm about Cetshwayo as their future king, he
offered my father his snuff-box with the remark: 'Good
snuff refreshes the heart and clears the head. The time has
come when we must keep a clear and cool head. You see,
I have come to make a suggestion to you.' Then, as if he
was searching for the right words, he too fell silent.

Z.17;
G.37-51 A young woman approached the two men on her
knees, carrying an earthenware vessel with beer. After
taking a sip as proof of its palatability and freedom from
harmful admixture, she passed the *khamba* to my father
who took a long and deep draught before passing the
drinking vessel to Maboya.

As if the foaming liquid had released his tongue, Maboya
resumed: 'I don't know if my heart will hurt your heart.
Look, I am concerned about the very man we have just

discussed — the crown prince! Cetshwayo has to enlarge his household — his *isigodlo*. We must build up his prestige among the people. He needs many helpers and servants at the royal residence — his *isigodlo* establishment must be enlarged.'

Quite innocently my father agreed, but enquired why Maboya regarded this as such an important matter and what suggestion he wished to make.

Maboya lowered his voice: 'Our clan, the Buthelezi, is also expected to dedicate some of its girls to the service of the future king. We must give up to him some of our best maidens, especially those of noble descent.'

With a sudden shock my father guessed what was in Maboya's mind; he paused, took a sip of beer and ventured: 'I don't suppose you have finished what you want to say.'

'No,' replied Maboya, 'I have not presented my request to you as yet.'

All my father managed to say flatly was, 'Continue, Buthelezi.'

After some hesitation Maboya Buthelezi then spoke clearly and with determination. 'The Buthelezi clan has decided to request you to dedicate your daughter, Nomguqo, to the service of the crown prince. She is still of tender years, but already comely and, as it is, also of royal descent. This gift will please the crown prince and enhance the goodwill and prestige we Buthelezis enjoy. Do we not already enjoy the trust that our Buthelezi girls are endowed with the privilege of preparing and serving all royal food?'

The thought that he should sacrifice his darling daughter by dedicating her to Cetshwayo's *isigodlo* was as unexpected as it was repugnant to my father, Sikhunyane, but he managed to control his inner feelings. A warning thought flashed through his mind: Be careful now with what you say! If the crown prince should learn that you were unwilling to give up your daughter to him, you might have to pay for this indiscretion with your life. He might even destroy the whole of your family. This matter has already been before the Buthelezi clan; you would never be able to hide your reluctance!

Sikhunyane's thoughts were in a turmoil; but he brought them under control; he dared not to reveal his indignation, but managed to reply: 'Buthelezi, you demand much of me. To dedicate the *inkosazana*, my favourite daughter, will mean to me that she no longer exists, that she will have passed out of my life. However, for the sake of our future king no sacrifice can be too great. I shall feel honoured that my daughter has been deemed fit to be dedicated to his service. I am prepared to acquiesce.'

Maboya Buthelezi responded with much relief: 'Dlamini Nkosi, you talk and act like a man. I thank you.'

The beer vessel having been drained and his purpose achieved, Maboya Buthelezi then prepared to leave. After some polite belching and an exchange of courtesies he rose, greeted and departed.

Baba Mhlahlela, I shall never forget that day and its foreboding of some fateful event. First there was this unusually long discussion between the *umnumzane*[22] and my father; then my father remained deep in thought and silence. We all seemed to sense that his were troubled thoughts.

Equally unforgettable remains the moment when sometime later, as I was about to leave his hut, my father called out, 'Stay, child, I have to tell you something of importance.'

I turned round with a startled look. My father had never spoken to me like this before. His voice was quite different and I became anxious.

Slowly my father began to speak: 'My daughter, I must speak to you, but don't become alarmed, You are almost still a child, yet you are already the comeliest amongst the maidens of this *umuzi*. I must now tell you that the counsellors of the Buthelezi clan have resolved that you, together with some Buthelezi girls, shall be destined to join the *isigodlo* of the crown prince.'

I looked up in surprise. My heart began to pound, I could hardly breathe. I stammered: 'Father, I . . . , I must go to the crown prince? I am still a child. Father, what does this mean?'

My father replied with quiet resolution: 'Nomguqo, it

is a great honour for you to have been selected to serve
the future king, to kneel before him in service. Go, my
child, go and serve the king with alertness and loyalty.'

The only reply I managed was to say, 'Father, I hear.'

I left the hut in confusion: I am to be given up to the
crown prince! What shall I do? I cannot run to my mother,
she lies in her grave. My heart grew heavy when I realised
that my life in our family home had come to an end.
No longer would I kneel at my father's hearth to kindle
the fire, no longer would I bring light to his hut in the
evenings by setting alight and holding stalks of grass in
innumerable succession. No longer would I associate with
my playmates; no longer be of service to my father; in
future I should have to kneel before the king.

Soon after, however, a surprising readiness to reassess
came over me: I am no longer just a child. I am deemed fit
and worthy to become a member of the king's court, to
be presented to his *isigodlo*. Great was the envy among my
half-sisters, when they heard the news. I can't recount all
the thoughts that passed through my mind during those
days. Yes, indeed, my childhood had come to an end. I
was facing a decisive change in my life.

OFF TO CETSHWAYO AT KHANDEMPEMVU

Z.18;
G.48-51

Baba Mhlahlela, you enquire after the progress of our
journey. There is not much I can tell. An early start was
made with the preparations for our journey. We were
supplied with all the necessaries. The bead ornaments
with requisite symbols were being made. New pieces of
cloth were acquired. Fresh ointments consisting of fats
and sweet-smelling herbs were prepared with which we had
to anoint our bodies and scent our cloth, in order to
dispense wafts of aromatic odours. Fat from the hippo-
potamus had to be procured. Applied to our faces this
would ensure that whoever beheld us would do so with
pleasure and benevolence. As the day of departure approached provisions for the journey, meat and mealie-

bread, were assembled.

On that memorable morning my father placed a special charm around my neck, which was to protect me on the journey to Khandempemvu, the residence of the crown prince. This *umuzi* was situated at the foot of the two Mabedlane hills not far from the great Inhlazatshe mountain and can be seen north-east from the Esibongweni mission station.

At the crack of dawn, when one can just discern the horns of cattle against the early morning sky,[23] we bade our farewell. Carrying all that we possessed on our heads, we moved off at a brisk pace and tarried nowhere. Anyone seeing our group would know that we were on our way to the crown prince's *umuzi*. We passed Ntabankulu[24] close to where the Bethel mission station now stands and then came to a heap of wishing stones [*isivivane*].[25] Each one of us picked up a stone along the footpath, spat on it and threw it on the *isivivane* to ensure good luck on our journey and a kind reception at the royal *umuzi*. We were thankful that no duiker[26] crossed our path, as that would have portended misfortune. On the other hand we were overjoyed to notice a yellowthroated longclaw, called *inqomfi*,[27] flying over us with a twitter several times. We acknowledged this sign of good fortune with happy words and laughter.

As we reached the royal *umuzi* on the following morning, an *induna* advised Cetshwayo of our arrival. My father, who had accompanied us, was soon admitted to the presence of the crown prince. Cetshwayo was obviously pleased that his father's fleetfooted messenger, whom he knew well, was prepared to give up to him his own daughter, and that his *isigodlo* would thereby be enriched by the addition of another maiden of noble descent. Orders were then given that we should be fed and well looked after.

Z.19;
G.52-54
Then came the moment when my father had to say good-bye to his *inkosazana* of fourteen or fifteen summers. This was a good-bye which, according to human reckoning, would be forever. Any girl or young woman who was taken into the *isigodlo* lost her freedom forever; there was no escape, for the *isigodlo* women were at all times strictly

supervised and guarded.

The parting was brief, but painful. I could hardly breathe when I entered the quarters of the younger girls, the *amatshitshi*. So I was one of them, but although young, I kept my eyes open and observed everything that went on at the *umuzi*.

It was at the beginning of the year in which old king Mpande died [1872] that we joined Cetshwayo's household. We actually visited Mpande before his death.

Z.20,21; However, we did not remain very long, not even a full
G.55-58 year, at this *umuzi*, since the crown prince soon removed to his other *umuzi*, Ndlangubo, near the Ngoye mountains. Whenever the crown prince moved about he had to be accompanied by a large group of *isigodlo* women, who had to carry his provisions and household goods and to attend to all manner of chores. I was also ordered to go along. Our duties were to plant and to harvest, to fetch water and firewood and perform all household tasks.

KWANDLANGUBO IN THE NGOYE MOUNTAINS

Z.22; Baba Mhlahlela, you said that you were interested to hear
G.56 something about my memories of life at kwaNdlangubo. I have particularly vivid memories of a white man, the missionary [Reverend] Schmidt,[28] an exceptionally big man. I feel quite ashamed now when I think how disrespectfully we girls of the *isigodlo* behaved towards him; but even some of the men showed little respect towards him. I understand that his predecessor and founder of the mission station at Endlangubo, Müller,[29] also had a rather hard time at that station. I was told that although Müller had to contend with many troubles, he was held in high esteem at the royal *umuzi*. A story told about him was that on his first visit to the king, when his audience had come to an end, he crawled backwards out of the hut. This was a breach of etiquette and an insult to the king. Immediately reproached by some upset *indunas*, who pointed out that, by crawling backwards, he appeared to

be distrusting the king,[30] Müller kept his composure and replied, 'Oh, King, I merely crawled backwards, because I wished to behold your noble countenance as long as possible.' Loud and approving laughter saved an otherwise embarrassing situation.

It was also said that the king ordered the execution of two men, who had behaved in an unseemly manner towards Müller. Müller's plea for mercy fell on deaf ears. Müller was deemed to be one of the king's men and as such the people were expected to treat him with deference.

His successor, Schmidt, also had his problems. We, the younger girls of the *isigodlo*, had to fetch the water needed at the royal *umuzi* from the Mhlathuzane river. The pathway we took led past the mission station and we always hankered after the lovely fruit we saw in the orchard. When the missionary saw us come, he took care that we did not enter the orchard. We would then surround him and call out in unison: '*Mlungu, akusiphe amapetshisi!*' [White man, give us peaches.] Others would then say: 'Give us that which can be eaten.'

Z.22;
G.59,60 He kept quiet when we behaved ourselves, but when we became unruly he would say, 'I shall report you to the prince.' The whole group would then retort, again in unison, 'We are not doing anything. Give us some red fruit, they look so nice, the red oranges and the lemons.' Quite often he would give us fruit and then say, 'Be gone!'

In his garden he also had prickly pears with particularly long thorns. Occasionally we would also sing out: '*Smiti, akusiphe ameva.*' [Schmidt, give us thorns.] 'Pick them yourselves,' was his reply. These thorns, which were very nice and long, we stuck into our hair and used them for extracting thorns from our feet. Yes, we really played the fool with him. For instance we would say in chorus, 'When will you return to your people overseas, so that we may eat from your garden that which is red?' He always kept quiet, presumably thinking that these girls were up to mischief again. He never became angry and was always of a kind and friendly disposition.

Z.23;
G.61-64 At that time he lived alone, but visited Cetshwayo frequently. People would say, 'Look there goes the king's white man.' He was given food.[31] Quite often, before the eyes of Cetshwayo, he would give this food to the people. Sometimes he took it home; young men would then be detailed to carry the meat for him. It would then happen quite often that the people would take the meat away from him, saying, 'Give it here.'

We teased him by singing in chorus words which previously had been directed at Müller:

> Siphe izingubo, weMele
> Wasinika ameva, weMele.
> Siphe izingubo!

> Give us clothes, oh Müller,
> You gave us thorns, oh Müller.
> Give us clothes!

There is nothing exciting I can tell you about the life at this *umuzi*. Life went by without any notable events. We fetched water, attending to planting and harvesting, and performed domestic duties in the huts of the royal wives.

However, there was another person, also a white man, who always gave us much to talk about. He was John Dunn,[32] a son-in-law of King Mpande who had, at any time, free access to the *isigodlo*. We called him Jantoni. There is much I will have to say about him.

KING MPANDE'S DEATH

z.24;
G.65-73

Baba Mhlahlela, a year went by without anything special having happened; but then a feeling of seriousness and expectation began to permeate our lives.

As the mealies ripened and harvesting time approached news reached us from the king's residence, Nodwengu, that '*Inkosi iyadunguzela*' [The king is indisposed]. This expression indicated, however, that something had happened which could not be spoken of in so many words, something which the men of the inner circle would know, but which

had to be kept away from the common people. Never-
theless it soon became known that the [seventy-four year]
old king, Mpande, had died.[33] We knew that following old
Zulu custom the body of the dead king had been bound up
in a squatting position and, wrapped in the hide of a
freshly slaughtered bull, was resting against one of the
uprights of his hut. Counsellors, *indunas*, in fact all inhabitants of the *umuzi* had to endure the stench of decom-
position. Only once the corpse had desiccated and become
odourless would it be buried. In order to endure the stench
people plugged their nostrils with crushed leaves of the
umsuzwane.[34] During this whole period it was said that
the king was 'indisposed'.

The burial of a Zulu king was a harrowing affair. Not
only would the articles last used by the deceased, such as
clothing, blankets, sleeping mats, eating utensils and
weapons[35] be interred with him, but his man-servant, one or
two wives and some *isigodlo* girls had to follow him into
the grave as well. And so it was also at King Mpande's
burial.

Even though it was said that Cetshwayo had declared
publicly, possibly to appease the British, that these hor-
rifying practices would not be followed at this burial,
he did in fact give orders that the king's body-servant[36]
and two of his wives should follow him into the spirit-
world. Those destined to follow a king into death had to
be killed. The victim had to be overpowered unexpectedly,
his mouth sealed and his neck broken. If he succeeded to
cry out, his life had to be spared.

The crown prince did not attend the burial in person.
His *indunas* insisted on his absence on the grounds that a
king should not go near a corpse.

Masiphula, the king's chief *induna*, conducted the
burial proceedings. However, he failed to comply with one
of Cetshwayo's orders, namely that Mpande's wife from
the Mthethwa clan should be one of those to be buried
with him. Moved by compassion he spared her life, but
thereby aroused Cetshwayo's anger. Of this, more later.

THE JOURNEY TO NODWENGU

Z.24;
G.71,72

In the meantime Cetshwayo was busy at his *umuzi*, making preparations for his journey into the interior to claim the Zulu throne. He was not sure whether some rivals would not contest his claim. Harvesting over, he began to move with his army.[37] The *isigodlo* girls had to join this march as they had to carry all the goods and chattels. The crown prince combined this march with a great hunt [*inqina*] demanded by the cleansing rites. The warriors had to wash their spears in blood to remove all the evil influences which the death of the king had brought upon them. Much game was slaughtered as we moved through the dense thornbush of the Mhlathuze valley.

On the second day we girls actually caught a big bush buck. As it jumped up in front of us, we dropped the loads we were carrying on our heads and rushed at it. We caught it eventually by its legs and some girls smashed its skull with pieces of wood. The buck cried pitifully. 'Meh! Meh!' We girls then screamed madly: 'Here is a buck! We caught it! We killed it!' Cetshwayo was greatly pleased and proclaimed: 'This is a good omen. Our road is clear. Our girls have caught and killed a wild animal – a ruminant, a bushbuck. Our girls have excelled the men!' On that day we were extolled as heroines. The bushbuck was skinned, grilled and consumed by the girls.

Z.24-27
G.73-75

When we reached the Emthonjaneni heights our soldiers pleased the crown prince immensely by killing a lion in a thicket. [At that time already a rare beast in those parts.] A camp was then pitched on the Emthonjaneni ridge. A large tent, which had been acquired for the purpose of this journey, accommodated the womenfolk. The soldiers erected emergency shelters. On the very first night a heavy rain set in. Throughout the night the soldiers sang one of Cetshwayo's praise songs, which dates back to the battle of the princes:

Nango-ke ozithulele.
Ji, kaqali muntu.

Behold the Silent-One.
Indeed, he doesn't quarrel with anyone.

At daybreak the sky began to clear; the mist rose and the sun came into its own, revealing before our eyes the great, broad valley of the kings, Emakhosini. In this valley Cetshwayo's great ancestors once lived and now lie buried. In shades of dun and brown, with a faint suggestion of dark green, the thorn-country stretched as far as the eye could see, merging with the Babanango mountains on the horizon. Somewhat to our left, to the south-west, were the low hills on which stood Mgungundlovu, where Piet Retief and his followers were killed and where also is situated the grave of the great ancestor, Zulu. He gave his name to the small and insignificant tribe from which great king Shaka emerged, he who brought together a host of small tribes and clans and amalgamated them into one mighty Zulu nation. Then our eyes were sent in the direction in which some other royal graves lay, those of Ndaba, Jama and others.[38] The location of the most sacred site, that of the *umuzi* called Nobamba,[39] was brought to our special attention. Zulus regard this 'Place of Unity and Strength' as the birthplace of their nation. It was here, too, that the magic coil, the *inkatha yezwe yakwaZulu*, symbol of Zulu unity and nationhood, was kept.[40] Not far distant from Nobamba and the grave of Senzangakhona, his grandfather, lay Makheni, the *umuzi* towards which Cetshwayo was heading. There he intended to bring sacrifices in order to make contact with the ancestral spirits and to appease them. Right in the centre of the valley is this hallowed spot where men must refrain from striking, or even touching the ground with their sticks, lest they disturb the spirits of those illustrious *abaphansi*.[41]

There was I, Nomguqo, looking across the valley and asking one of the Buthelezi girls if she knew in which direction the ancient home of the Buthelezi lay. She let my eyes travel along the horizon to the mountains in the north-west to an area where, as I know today, the mission station, Esibongweni, is situated. Obviously I did not foreknow that a day would come when, right here in the heart of Zululand, I would work and serve as a disciple of that King of Kings, Jesus Christ.

Z.27;
G.76
It must have been part of God's design that, as an adolescent, I should first have experienced and observed all the darkness of paganism evident even at the grand court of the Zulu king. I was to become a witness to all the awfulness, the injustices and cruelties of witchcraft and sorcery, so that I would later be able to proclaim to my people the righteousness and peace of God with greater conviction and joyful determination.

Z.28,29
G.77,78
The first few days at Emthonjaneni were filled with anxious suspense: there was much talk of war. Not everybody in the country was well-disposed towards Cetshwayo. Cetshwayo himself expected opposition from his late father's capital *umuzi*; but even the inhabitants of that royal *umuzi*, on their part, were filled with anxiety and fear. They believed that Cetshwayo's advent would end in an armed confrontation. The tension was greatly eased by the arrival of Theophilus Shepstone, whom we called Somtsewu.[42] Cetshwayo had advised him of the death of the King, and Somtsewu had now come to crown him as the new king. Somtsewu, on his own initiative, had also taken the precaution to spread the message that Cetshwayo had no belligerent intentions, and that the people should have no fear. As a matter of fact, all further events developed peacefully. We left Emthonjaneni and, descending into the valley, moved to Makheni.[43] The people from Nodwengu came to meet the future king with a large herd of cattle. Anxiety and fear subsided. Heart and happiness returned. Every day large numbers of cattle were slaughtered and, with an abundance of meat, we lived in grand style.

At Makheni, an old and memorable royal *umuzi*, Cetshwayo met his obligations towards his ancestral spirits to ensure that under their auspices he, his throne and his people would be bound together in a mystic community of spirit; this would augur well for the kingship he was about to enter. As part of the ritual for the spiritual and magic induction of the new king, twenty head of cattle were sacrificed. These were first driven to Nobamba to be imbued with the magical spirit of the *inkatha*, the sacred symbol of Zulu unity and strength.

Z.30;
G.79,80
During our sojourn at Makheni the suitability of a number of localities for the erection of a new royal *umuzi* was explored. Finally a stretch of thorn-country to the north of the White Mfolozi river was selected. The site on which the King's new *umuzi*, to be called Ondini,[44] would arise was situated between the two older royal *imizi*, Nodwengu and Mlambongwenya. At the latter, specially erected for her, still lived the late King Mpande's mother, Songiya, born Ngotsha of the Hlabisa clan. An immediate start was made with clearing the area. The thorn trees were felled and all brushwood burnt. In great haste emergency shelters were erected in order that the actual coronation, to which everybody looked forward full of eager expectation, could proceed.

Soon after, Cetshwayo moved off to the new site and arrived there at the same time as Shepstone.[45] When we arrived, work on the provisional shelters was still in progress.

Z.31, 32;
G.81
Then, at the nearby Mlambongwenya, where the nation had assembled, Cetshwayo was proclaimed King of the Zulus. When the people had assembled Shepstone stood up in their midst and called out: 'Men of the Zulu nation! Behold your king! I have come to enthrone him, because Mpande has designated him as his successor by making a mark on his right ear. Here now is your king whom I have delivered into your midst. Do not ever harm him.'

Z.33;
G.82
There was military music and a crashing of drums. Everybody rose and gave praise. The midday sun was scorchingly hot. The warriors danced and sang the king's praises:

> Nango-ke ozithulele.
> Ji, kaqali muntu.

> Behold the Silent-One.
> Indeed, he doesn't quarrel with anyone.

The noise was quite frightening, almost as if there was thunder in the sky.

Shepstone received a gift of cattle and a few days

later took his leave. The ceremony made a deep impression on me.

BUILDING THE ROYAL RESIDENCE — ONDINI

Z.34
G.83

After the coronation the building activites on the new site at Ondini were resumed with feverish haste. The populace had been directed to procure much high-quality building materials. The women had to supply thatch and plaited grassropes. The men had to proceed to the virgin forests to search for long straight saplings for the wicker frames of the huts. These long, smooth laths were obtained by the Khandempemvu and Gobamakhosi regiments from the Nkandla forest. Good clay-soil for the floors of the huts had to be found and this again the women had to fetch, carrying it on their heads. The medicine-men had to apply a variety of magical substances and medicines to protect the new *umuzi* against all harm and evil.[46]

Z.35
G.84-86

The royal huts were separated from the remainder of the *umuzi* by a high fence. These huts were again sub-divided into two divisions by another fence. One was called the *isigodlo esimnyama* [the black *isigodlo*]. This division contained the king's private hut, the huts of his wives and mothers[47] and the élite of the *isigodlo* girls, known as the *umndlunkulu*, who waited upon the royal wives or were at the disposal of the king as concubines. Only the king had access to this division; an unauthorised person found therein would forfeit his life.

The other subdivision was called the *isigodlo esimhlophe* [the white *isigodlo*]. It contained the huts of the royal children and the remainder of the *isigodlo*, the younger girls and those who had not drawn the attention of the king.

Behind this fence, which separated the white *isigodlo* from the huts of the warriors, a small mound had been formed from the top of which the king could overlook the whole *umuzi*. Similarly, a mound had been formed behind the windbreak of his own private hut from which he could overlook and watch the whole *isigodlo* area.[48]

Z.36-38
G.87

A square house built with bricks was also erected for the king. It was called the *indlu 'mnyama* [black house]. The building material was supplied by a Norwegian missionary whom we called Mondi.[49] The actual construction was undertaken by Johannes Ntuli, son of Jwangubane Ntuli, and two other Zulu converts of the Norwegian mission. One day, when building operations were in full swing, we had a rather unnerving experience. The king had detailed two of the girls to see to the feeding of these building workers. Although there was an abundance of supplies, it so happened that mealtime had passed by without the builders having been given their food. The king chanced to pass by and asked the men whether they had eaten. One of them replied: 'No, *inkosi*,[50] we have not eaten as yet; the girls don't seem to have cooked; but there is food around.' When the two young women were asked for an explanation they were unable to utter a sound. The one was born a Mngadi and the other a Mbatha. Both were adults and knew what was expected of them. The king had them executed forthwith. He ordered that they should pay for their omission by 'being married to the bewhiskered man at the *Nkatha*'.[51] That both had to pay with their lives on the same day shocked and frightened us. We did not consider their neglect of duty sufficiently severe to merit the death penalty.

Z.38
G.88

This 'black house' was rectangular. It had four rooms with two outside doors and windows.[52] The king used one room as a place where he spent part of the day and where he met his counsellors and *indunas* and attended to the affairs of state. At night the doors were locked and the house was guarded by two girls who were the keepers of the keys. The king slept in his private hut.

Z.35,39
G.89

The royal *isigodlo* had three gate openings. One was reserved for the 'mother' who looked after the king. His own mother, Ngqumbazi, a daughter of Tshana Zungu, was no longer alive at that time. Another opening was used by the other mothers, whose names I no longer remember. The main entrance was used by the king, his body servants who also lived there, and all his *isigodlo* girls. The white man, John Dunn, whom I shall mention again, also had free access at any time through this opening. What a beautiful *umuzi* this was! We lived here for five years; but in the sixth year it was destroyed by the British.

CETSHWAYO'S MAGIC COIL — THE *INKATHA*

Z.40;
G.90

Right in the centre of the black *isigodlo* was situated a most sacred shelter called *eNkatheni* — a hut containing Cetshwayo's personal *inkatha* and the nation's *inhlendla*, a ceremonial barbed assegai. Anyone passing through the entrance to the white *isigodlo* would face the entrance to the black *isigodlo* and would see beyond that the door-opening leading into the shelter. The common people were not permitted even to mention the *inkatha*. Talking about it was as much taboo[53] as the singing of certain national songs, which were sung only on the occasion of important national feasts in the presence of the chiefs. Only on the occasion of great feasts was the *inkatha* brought into the open; at all other times it would remain in the hut. A venerable old woman was appointed as guardian. The king went into this hut when he wished to discuss matters of national importance, or when great feasts were being celebrated. In these latter instances the king had to perform ceremonial ablutions while sitting on the *inkatha*. The young men who attended to the king on these occasions were Mehlokazulu Ngobese, Nsizwana Xulu and the two sons of Mnyamana Buthelezi, Tshanibezwe and Mbulawa. They took turns to fetch the king's washing and drinking water from Hlopekhulu. The water for washing was poured into an earthen vessel and whirled with a three-pronged twirling-stick. A 'royal' herb added to the water caused it to foam. The king would wash himself with the water and rub the foam into the skin. Any remaining water had to remain inside the hut; mixed with cow-dung it would be smeared over the floor of the hut, which would then be polished over again. We girls were sometimes naughty, surreptitiously peeping into the hut to see what was going on inside.

Z.41;
G.91

The magic coil of the *inkatha* was so big and wide that the king could squat on it. It was intertwined with grass and wrapped round with some new cloth. Its contents symbolised the unity of the nation and all the values associated with the king's ancestors. The properties and magic prowess of wild animals embodied in this coil were transferred through it to the people. Shaka greatly strengthened the power of the *inkatha.* He subjected a large number of tribes but formed them into a united people by collecting bits from the *izinkatha* of vanquished tribes and particles from the bodies of slain chiefs and embodying them in his own coil.

Z.41;
G.92

When the king has made physical contact with the *inkatha*, when he sits on it, a power emanates from him which transcends all distance. He can influence his army so that it does not waver and stands united in battle to defeat the enemy. He also prevents the spirits of dead chiefs and their followers, from aiding the enemy in battle, because when he sits on his *inkatha*, holding the ceremonial assegai, those spirits become a footrest for his feet. This assegai, the *inhlendla* takes the place of a sceptre. It is crescent-shaped and has a long shaft.

Z.41;
G.93

This magic coil also has the effect that a fugitive cannot make good his escape if any article belonging to him or her is placed on it. When Jikijiki, the daughter of Sigodo Mnguni fled, some of her belongings were placed on the *inkatha* and she was duly caught.

Z.45;
G.94

The medicine-man who was responsible for treating Cetshwayo's *inkatha* was Dlephu Ndlovu. He came from Emakhabeleni [in the Umsinga district] and belonged to the Zondi of the Bambatha clan. He was also the medicine-man who installed Cetshwayo on his *inkatha* when he, for the first time as king, performed the ceremony of the 'First Fruits'.[54]

THE ZULU FESTIVAL *INKOSI ISHAYA USELWA*

Z.47;
G.95

In connection with the 'First Fruits' the Zulu people celebrated two festivals at which the warriors would appear in full war-dress. The 'little' and the 'big' festival were both celebrated with much pomp and circumstance. Shortly before the time when we now celebrate Christmas, that is before the summer solstice, the 'little' festival, called *ulwezi* or *inkosi ishaya uselwa* [the king squirts out calabash concoction], was celebrated; then, a month or two later, followed the 'big' festival, called *uzibandlela*, at which the king would proclaim his laws.[55]

Z.48;
G.96-98

I wish to tell some more about the 'little', yet important feast, which left a greater impression on me than the crowning of the king by Shepstone. At this Feast of the First Fruits there were two important features: not only was the king enthroned according to Zulu custom, but he and the nation were strengthened and rejuvenated by a revitalising of the *inkatha*.

After Shepstone's departure, following the coronation, the fields were cultivated and the construction of the royal *umuzi* completed. In good time the young men were sent down to the coastal areas to collect all the calabashes, [*izinselwa*][56] needed for the feast, as also quantities of a fibrous plant, called *imizi*,[57] which would be used in making a festive garment for the king.

In addition, the young men had to move through the country to collect substances which were believed to embody the power and energy of the nation. These 'soul-substances' were found in the 'body dirt' of the populace, but especially that of chiefs and the king himself. Tiny bits of grass against which the feet of passing multitudes had brushed on the country's footpaths, samples of thatch or scrapings from the wooden posts from doorways against which people had rubbed in crawling in and out of huts, and scrapings from any article with which friend or foe had been in physical contact, all these contained the essence of the soul of the nation or a means by which the enemies of the nation could be suppressed. Small samples of these specimens were then incorporated in the magic coil whereby the soul of the nation, represented by it, became enlarged, strengthened and rejuvenated.

Z.49;
G.99
 In preparation for the festival special songs and dances were practised by us girls, and by the men separately. Our songs were different from those of the men. We practised in particular a song, *Woza nkosi, woza lapha!* [Come, Oh King, come hither!]. This was the principal song we had to sing at the coming festival. We were being instructed by the women from the *umuzi* of the late king, Mpande.

Z.50;
G.100
 Shortly before the festival some wagons arrived from John Dunn, whom we called Jantoni, and brought goods for the king. They brought coffee, sugar, salt, bananas, beads and colourful cloths which were to provide festive raiment for big and small.

Z.51-53;
G.100
 Then the king ordered all the young women to assemble according to their regiments.[58] The Amaqwaki regiment came first, then the Amadlundlu, then the Amaduku, then the Inkwelembe, then in fifth place the Izijinga. I belonged to this fifth regiment composed of girls in their teens. The first regiment received cloths of the same colour. The king's stewards distributed the blankets, cloths and beads. Everyone was considered, because none of the girls could be left empty-handed on this day. After these gifts had been distributed the king was praised with the words, 'Ndabezitha, lord of the nation, we thank thee!'[59] We then adorned ourselves with all the colourful cloths and beads.

Z.54-56;
G.101
 The days went by with practising. Wood was being collected for brewing beer. A colossal amount of germinated sorghum grain[60] was ground as malt. Now everybody knew on what day the festival would take place. On the day before the feast the young men crushed the fibrous plants and the older men wove them into a garment for the king.

Z.56;
G.102
 The feast began in the late afternoon. All the regiments, the royal wives and the maidens commenced singing a festive song, glorifying the king. The words of the king's song were as follows:

Nguwe Dlambula,
Nguwe Mswazi!
Siyakubahlula ngezikhali,

Abahambi 'bakhona
Benjengezulu liduma.

It is you, Dlambula,
It is you, Mswazi!
We shall overcome them with weapons,
Those that are there,
As vast as the heaven when it thunders.

This song was permitted to be sung only on the occasion of this feast, and it became banned again on the day following the feast. Anyone singing it thereafter would have lost his life.

Z.58;
G.103

Not one of the girls slept on that night. In rival sing-songs we contended for the king. Each regiment tried to get hold of him. We surrounded him, like bees congregating around their queen; we called out to him, attempting to lead him our way. He was then in the wives' section of the *isigodlo.* Soon after he withdrew to his hut and was not seen again until the following morning. But this did not stop us from calling out to him in our song, 'Come, Oh King, come here to us.'

Z.59;
G.104

Throughout this night a light was kept burning in the hut harbouring the magic coil. At sunrise the king emerged from this hut, his face painted in three colours, the right cheek white, the forehead red and the left cheek pitch black. He was wrapped up in the greenish covering made of fibre. His whole body from head to toes was enshrouded by it; only his face showed. He looked like a big tree, nay, like a monster. From all quarters he was assailed with shouts, 'Come here, come this way, Oh King!' How we did shout when, at sunrise, he emerged from the hut, the sacred spear, the *inhlendla*, in his right hand! The crescent-shaped blade of the spear, resembling the new moon, gleamed in the rays of the early morning sun. The king then left the black *isigodlo* followed by all the women and maidens.

Z.60-62;
G.105

In the meantime the male regiments had assembled in their ceremonial attire: the Khandempemvu, then its corresponding age group, the Mboza, to whom the Indluyengwe was affiliated, the Uve, the Ngobamakhosi, and the recently raised Falaza regiment, which belonged to my own age group. The approaching troops were in a bellicose mood. It almost came to a clash between the warriors because each group tried to claim the king for itself; but the parties were appeased before an open fight could develop.

When all the regiments, resplendent in their war-dress, had taken up their position the royal salute, *Bhayede nkosi!*[61] thundered forth from many a thousand throats.

Z.62; G.106 The king then raised his sceptre and his right foot and gave the order to commence the *ngoma.*[62] All the regiments, the royal wives and the *isigodlo* maidens raised their voices and swayed their bodies to participate in the national song-dance peculiar to the First Fruits festival:

> It is you, Dlambula,
> It is you, Mswazi!
> We shall overcome them with weapons,
> Those that are there,
> As vast as the heaven when it thunders.

One regiment after another then moved forward to present its song-dance. The Khandempemvu regiment had precedence. Adorned with snow-white oxtails they began to sing and dance:

> Wena weNdlovu enamandla,
> Akusiphe impi!
> Izizwe zonke zishona enhla,
> Ziya kwaMshelekwane
> Izizwe zonke, Mshweshwe, ziyakwala.
> AmaBhunu ayabaleka;
> Akusiphe impi.
> Izizwe zonke zishona enhla!
> Ayabaleka amaBhunu,
> Ashona lenhla kwaMshelekwane.

> You mighty elephant,
> Give us war!
> All nations disappear to the north,
> They go to Mshelekwane.

> All nations hate you, Mshweshwe, [Cetshwayo]
> The Boers take to flight;
> Give us war.
> All nations disappear to the north.
> The Boers are running,
> They flee northwards to Mshelekwane.[63]

Z.64
G.107

When this regiment had taken up its position, the royal wives and the maidens had to emerge from the *isigodlo* singing:

> Wayiwa — wo, wo, wo —
> Izizwe, wena nkosi,
> Bakuncishile.
> Lala phansi.
> Inkube yendlala imbi!

> You have been treated with disdain — wo, wo, wo —
> By the nations, Oh King;
> They have treated you niggardly.
> Lie down.
> The famine is bad indeed.

Z.65, 66
G.108

While one regiment was singing and dancing, the others were eating and drinking. Towards midday the regiments were called upon to kill the biggest and meanest bull that could be found, with their bare hands. It had to be over-powered and then its neck had to be broken. At the last festival in which I participated the bull nearly got away from the warriors. Finally the Udududu regiment succeeded in twisting and breaking its neck, but only after it had gored two soldiers to death.

Z.67, 68
G.109

The bull was not skinned but cut up into strips and pieces. A portion of the meat was eaten by the young men who had tanned the fibrous plants for the king's festive garment. Strips of meat were roasted, treated with medicine and thrown into the air. The warriors had to catch them, suck at them without swallowing, spit out and pass them on. The men were not permitted to eat any of the meat. The remaining meat and all bones, except the sinews, were burnt to ash. The sinews were used in renewing the magic coil. Ash is one of the ritual remedies of our people. You will know, Baba Mhlahlela, that you will never be presented with meat containing bones, for instance, from a beast slaughtered at a wedding. Care is always taken to retain the bones of such a beast at the *umuzi*, where they are burnt to ash and used as medicine.

After the bones of the bull had been burnt to ash, the medicine-men had to grind the ash and cinders into a fine powder. The great national medicine-man and personal physician of the king, Dlephu Ndlovu from Emakhabeleni, whom I have already mentioned, added to this ground ash pulverised particles from wild animals, special plants, and the 'body dirt' or soul-essence of the living nation, as collected by the young men. This mystic black powder was the nation's magic medicine; it rejuvenated and united, it could be used offensively or defensively; it was an important medicinal addition to the *inkatha* and would protect the king and the nation against all evil and enemy action. The whole army was doctored with water to which some of this magic powder had been added, to enhance its courage and prowess and to protect it against any evil influences.

Z.68
G.110
The final act involved the gourds. Sitting on the magic coil, the king dipped his finger into the black powder, licked it, and then spat out a mighty spray. He then picked up the gourds and threw them at the soldiers who had to break off small pieces and put them in their mouths.

Z.69
G.111
With this act the new year was proclaimed. From now on the people were allowed to eat from the new season's crops. From now on the reed pipes could also be played again, after they had remained silent for many months. In the late afternoon the multitude assembled for communal singing and dancing. Wonderful, yet awe-inspiring, was the singing of the national songs. With great enthusiasm did the dancing proceed. One of the dances was accompanied by a chorus pronouncing:

> Bayamzonda bonk' abantu.
> No Sobhuza uyamzonda;
> No Mswazi uyamzonda.
> Zonk' izizwe ziyamzonda!

All the people hate him.
Sobhuza also hates him;
Mswazi also hates him.
All the nations hate him!

Z.70
G.112
    Late in the evening the festivities came to an end. The king first went into the hut harbouring the magic *inkatha,* which was being guarded by one of the 'mothers'. Then the king went into a hut close by where he spent the night. No one could see the king. The royal mothers guarded this hut. On this night he abstained from the *isigodlo* girls. It was said, 'The king is fasting!'

Z.71
G.113
    On the following morning he put ornaments made of bushy tails on his arms and legs. The fibre garment was burnt. As an end to the festivities general ablutions were prescribed. The soldiers went to bathe in one river, and we women in another. This symbolic cleansing brought the festival to an end.

Z.73, 76
G.114
    These festivals were also attended by white men – missionaries – whom we called *abafundisi.* They brought presents for the king. There was, for instance, a Norwegian missionary [Reverend Gundersen] whom we called Guniseni. He was very tall. Because he and his wife were childless the king presented him with a girl, who was to be both servant and daughter. I knew this girl, but have forgotten her name. When this girl eventually got married, the *lobola* cattle were received by the missionary. Cetshwayo received regular visits from this missionary. The king was secretly intrigued by the Christian belief. However, he concealed this fact from the people, because he feared that he would be ridiculed if it became known that he was being taught. He loved to listen to the missionaries relating stories of the Lord; but his heart remained hard, because he was afraid that he might lose his crown. He refrained from expounding any views on these matters in public.

Z.74
G.115
    Another white man was an Englishman, Jantoni Simdoni [John Dunn]. We also addressed him as *umfundisi*, although he was not a missionary. His [principal] wife was Catherine of the Fihlaswe people.[64] Jantoni was a good-looking man. Later on he became a polygamist. He was living on the

coast. Every year shortly before Christmas he arrived in an ox-wagon loaded with gifts for the king, such as sugar, salt, coffee, blankets, etc. Cetshwayo held him in high esteem and gave him Zulu girls in marriage. To begin with he gave him girls from one of the royal *imizi* close to the coast. Among these were Cetshwayo's own sisters, Sobejile, daughter of Phalane, born Mkhwanazi; and the other, daughter of Sigodi, born Mguni. Cetshwayo bestowed on him a portion of his realm, from Eshowe to the Ngoye mountains. The friendship between these two men was so close that Cetshwayo later on even gave girls from his upper royal *umuzi* as wives to John Dunn. Cetshwayo even had *imizi* built for these wives of Jantoni, within the area bestowed on him, as his brother-in-law. At each *umuzi* he established two of these wives. John Dunn ruled over his domain and raised a countless progeny of mixed blood. When he visited Cetshwayo he usually stayed for a month and spent much time telling stories about the world across the seas.

EVERYDAY LIFE AT ONDINI

Z.77-82
G.116-118

After the festival we returned to ordinary, everyday life. Every day brought some joy or sorrow. An ordinary workday began at the break of dawn when the gatekeeper called out the *izibongo*,[65] the praises of the king. We had to rise forthwith, tidy the huts and sweep the yard. At sunrise the king emerged from his hut. By that time everything had to be tidy and orderly. As soon as he appeared his manservants came forward; if the king wished to go on an early morning hunt, they fetched the sporting guns from the 'black house'. When he left, the whole *umuzi* appeared as if deserted, yet it was full of people; but no one was allowed to show himself. Many birds were shot and brought home. He usually returned when the sun already stood high in the sky. That was then also the time for him to go out to a nearby hillock. Then he would proceed to a neat enclosure of prettily executed lattice-work to perform his ablutions.

The young men fetched his bathwater from the Mbilane stream which arose in nearby hills. This water was poured into an earthenware vessel. The king's drinking water came from a cold and bubbling spring on Hlophekhulu mountain. The king was rubbed down by the same young men who had fetched the water. They were also the same men who attended to him when he was seated on the magic coil: Mehlokazulu Ngobese, Nsizwana Xulu, and the two sons of Mnyamana, Tshanibezwe and Mbulawa. They took turns in pairs to attend to the king for one month at a time. During his ablutions the king stood on a stone. He stood silent, and a deadly silence reigned over the whole *umuzi*; but we girls were naughty, we peeped through the lattice-work of the enclosure and admired his magnificent physique. After the ablution he sat on the stone until he was dry. He then put on his *beshu* [buttock-covering] of leopard skin, went to his hut in the black *isigodlo* and called for food.

Z.83
G.119-
123
When the king was about to partake of a meal, two of his grooms would move around the *umuzi*, calling out, '*Ungathinti!*', meaning literally, 'Don't disturb!', but also meaning that no one was permitted to cough. One of the manservants would walk round one side of the *umuzi*, the second one on the other side, all the time calling out '*Ungathinti!*'. Everyone then knew that the king was eating and that coughing was prohibited. When I suffered an attack of asthma during such times, I had to leave the *umuzi*, together with others who felt a need to cough, and we remained outside the *umuzi* until the king had finished eating, even if this was at night-time. When the king had finished eating somebody usually called us, saying that we could now return. My asthma became more troublesome during cold weather. A little alcoholic liquor which the king then gave me brought some relief. If I had no asthma there was no need for me to leave the *umuzi*. I then had to assist in guarding the area in which the king's food was kept and prepared. The hut in which the king's food was stored was called Ohlangeni.

Before a meal, the girls who had prepared the food, had to take water to the king for washing his hands. It was left to the girls from the Buthelezi clan to prepare the king's food and to guard the food-store and the cooking area. The king placed greater trust in these girls than in other men or women. The girls who did the actual cooking took turns.

After the king had washed his hands, a whole string of girls came into motion. Sliding on their knees they presented the king with his food. Other indispensable items had to be presented in the same manner: a spoon, a fly-whisk, and a finely-woven mat on which the food-dishes were deposited. His favourite foods were *amasi* [sour milk] and meat. He would first eat the sour, curdled milk and thereafter the meat. After the meat, sorghum beer was brought in and consumed until late into the night.

Having completed his own meal, the king then handed food out to the young men and women who had served him, quite often in unmanageable quantities. When I was well I had a good appetite and managed to finish the food apportioned to me. If we had been given too much food, we could under no circumstance pass it on to someone else unless we had secured the king's permission. It was part of the procedure that the king would ask, 'Is there someone nearby who might help you eating?' One had to reply quickly, 'Yes, Ndabezitha!' The king would then allocate the food to such other person. Failure to follow this polite procedure might lead to the imposition of a fine of one beast.

When the supply of meat neared its end, this fact was reported to the king, who then ordered that *inyoni ephumile* [the bird which has flown] should be brought in to be killed. *Inyoni ephumile* was a euphemism for the next beast which was to be killed. If it was found that the slaughtered beast was too lean, this was reported to the king; then another one had to be slaughtered.

Z.84
G.132
To round off the picture of everyday life I must mention the king's sanitary arrangements. Whenever he wished to pass water, he relieved himself behind his hut in an area set aside for the purpose. But in winter when it was cold, or when it rained, he called for a chamber-pot and used it in the presence of the people and the girls. When he wanted to go to stool, he put on a black overcoat with red facing

on collar and sleeves, a black hat and shoes and then went
out to some high ground nearby.

THE KING'S CHARACTER

Z.86
G.124
Cetshwayo took after his mother, Ngqumbazi, born
Zungu. He was a big, heavily built man, with a firm body.
There was nothing soft about him. His younger brother,
Silwane, was of medium height. His half-brother, Hamu,
was also very big, but his body was soft and corpulent. Our
king was very good-looking and of royal demeanour.

Z.87
G.125
He was greatly concerned with the affairs of his people.
The people had ready access to him and he listened attent-
ively. He was not rash in condemning people to death; but
he did order executions on quite a number of occasions.
Masiphula, who had been Mpande's chief councellor, was
always quick at hand to have people killed; but Cetshwayo
often intervened and prevented this.

Z.88
G.126
Our king tended to be rather taciturn. For this reason he
was referred to in many of his *izibongo* [praises] as
'*Uzithulele*' [the Silent-One]. At other times he could be
very cheerful and his merry thoughts and witticisms raised
many a laugh. However, when he became angry, nobody
dared oppose him.

Z.89, 90
G.127
Cetshwayo was very stingy. He had inherited this trait
from his mother, Ngqumbazi Zungu, who had a reputation
of never ever offering anyone a drink of beer. His wife,
Unomvimbi, daughter of Msweli Mnguni, and the mother
of his heir, Dinuzulu, was also very stingy. Cetshwayo did
not distribute food readily; only after it had been reported
to him that the people were hungry was food released. On
the other hand, we girls never went hungry. We shared his
food and surreptitiously kept some. He received supplies of
amadumbe,[66] sweet potatoes, potatoes, bananas and pine-
apples. Much of it rotted away because he alone could not
eat it all; but he would not allow it to be distributed, until
it was reported to him that these foodstuffs were perishing.
Only then did he order that the people should receive some.

Excess supplies were then dished out to various huts. Then the people ate and became satisfied. They then approached his quarters and proclaimed their gratitude.

Z.91-93
G.128,
130
But the people had an opportunity to bring home to the king what they thought of his stinginess and bias. It was a Zulu custom that on the occasion of the wedding between the king and his principal wife, the wedding dance-song could contain allusions to the king's weaknesses and short-comings, which, on this occasion, he had to accept in good humour and without taking offence. The wedding dance-song [*isigekle*] was sung by a leader and chorus, accompanied by the clapping of hands. The dance was performed by the groom's party. While still at Ngoye, following an arrangement made by his father, Mpande, Cetshwayo had taken as his principal wife Nompaka, daughter of Sekethwayo Mdlalose. She was also known as Usixipe and was the mother of Princess Beyisile. The dance-song recounted his weaknesses and annoyed him greatly. Though vexed he had to smile, because he was not allowed to get angry; but he said that he was being maligned.

He guessed correctly that the song had been composed by his brother, Dabulamanzi, and not by Mshwankele Ngcobo, who normally composed wedding songs and who had practised the song and accompanying dance with us. The words were as follows:

Chorus
Hloma sihambe
Liyaphendula
Ayiya, buyisani abantwana benu
Liyaphendula. Khwishi mbo!

Song-leader
Nigsho oNgayiyane
Ngisho eliqoma lonkana
Ethi elikanina. Khwishi mbo!

Uthuli lwezichwe
Lapha zibanga ilanga
Zithi gebu qethu, zithi gebu qethu. Khwishi mbo!

Intaba yamaQongqo
Imhlophe ngamathambo yamadoda
Kuwe Zikhali. Khwishi mbo!

Chorus

Song-leader
Insingizi emlom' ebomvu
Uxamu wesiziba
Usathatha aphonseke. Khwishi mbo!

Yeka isixoshwa 'kudla.
Siyona izindaba.
Sithat' amehlo
Siwafaka phakathi emagobongweni
Sengathi angaholwa ngemuva. Khwishi mbo!

Untuluntulu
Onganqathaza-mbuzi
Siyayivuthela
Asaza yakhotha.
Azikhothe. Sibone? Khwishi mbo!

Chorus

Song-leader
Ishalashala leli lombheka phansi
Elidla lingabelisabheka.
Uyaphana-ke khona sibheka!

Okwalo-ke uholokoqo lolu
Olumhlandla ungango wengwenya
Yek' isisu amabhuku.
Imiphand' ibhulawa yizakhelani. Khwishi mbo!

Yebo, sakubona, sakubeletha,
Ngehleka lingaphethe lá kithi
Mgodoyi, lidle libe lingasabheka
Lithi lingaphatha isinqindi.

Lithi liyasebenza
Lisafuna amaseko,
Sibheka.

Ishalashala leli
Lombheka phansi
Lidla lingasabheki. Khwishi mbo!

The approximate meaning is as follows:

Chorus
Take up arms! Let us go!
The weather is changing.
Come on, bring your children back.
The weather is changing. Whirlwind ho!

Song-leader, accompanied by the clapping of hands
I mean him, Ngayiyane and his people.[67]
I mean him, who claims the world,
Saying, it belongs to his mother. Whirlwind ho!

Whirlwind of the Bushmen.[68]
When they darken the sun,
Raising dust with shuffling feet. Whirlwind ho!

The Drakensberg mountains
Gleam white with the bones of men
There you are, Zikhali![69] Whirlwind ho!

Chorus

Song-leader
Hornbill with the red beak!
Monitor lizard from the deep pool,
Throwing itself into the water,
As soon as it has taken its food. Whirlwind ho!

Leave this food-chaser alone![70]
He spoils all things.
He takes his eyes,
And hides them in the sockets of his eyes,
As if retracted from behind![71] Whirlwind ho!

Babbler, who promises much,
But gives nothing.
In vain do we incite him
To accept us. Will we ever find
That he will feed us?[72] Whirlwind ho!

Chorus

Song-leader
This unsociable person, this down-looker,[73]
Who when he eats, never looks around!
Oh, how open-handed, when we look on!

This is the way of this slender person;
His spine, like that of a crocodile.[74]
Note the mighty stomach.
From him worst harm may be expected![75]
Whirlwind ho!

Yes, we saw you, we carried you on our backs,
Miser, who laughs only when he is not eating.[76]
Scamp, no looking up, when he's engrossed in eating.
He thinks that when he holds a blade
He is already working.
He is searching for hearth-stones,
When we look on.
This unsociable person, this down-looker,
When he eats, he has no time for anyone else.
Whirlwind ho!

Z.94
G.128,
131

It was a wild dance and the wedding guests were bubbling over with delight. Cetshwayo managed to conceal his annoyance and put up a pleasant front. This was made easier for him by the fact that Nompaka [Wild Cat] was a splendid bride. When Mpande gave away this bride to Cetshwayo, he also granted him the right to wear the Zulu head-ring as a visible sign of his dignity on having entered a man's estate.

A PUBERTY CEREMONY

Z.95-97
G.133

We undertook many things at the royal residence of which, having since then become a disciple of our Lord Jesus Christ, I now feel honestly ashamed. At the time, however, there were practices and celebrations which gave us much joy and pleasure. There was, for instance, the *umgonqo* [puberty ceremony] at the royal *umuzi*, which Cetshwayo wished to be arranged for Nobathwa, daughter of Mbambisi, who had reached the required age. The preparation for and the celebration itself kept us occupied for quite some time. The girl's father had been one of Cetshwayo's *izinduna* at his Esiqhageni residence near Eshowe. But because Mbambisi Nala had associated with the royal wives, the king had him killed. He was betrayed by some men who disliked him and was killed near Eshowe. However, Cetshwayo had ordered the executioners to bring back with them any of the victim's daughters, no matter how young they were, because he knew that they were pretty. Their father had been a magnificent, good-looking man. And so the executioners returned with four girls: Nobathwa, Usiyobi, Unozizwe and Unoyibanga. The four wives of the *induna* were spared and allowed to remain at Esiqhageni. Thus this man had to die because he had shared food with the royal wives, and because he was hated by some men.

Z.98
G.134

The *umgonqo* celebration of Nobathwa was handled by some of the older girls. I still remember their names; they were Umafutha and Noyinkuni, both daughters of Qethuka; Noyifamona, daughter of Godide Ntuli; Nobhodlile, a third daughter of Qethuka, and Nguyaze, called Sala, who was a sister of Sibamu.

Z.99-103
G.135-
136

Nobathwa was confined to a special hut for a period of three months, during which period we other girls had to provide her with company. Only in the fourth month was she permitted to leave the hut.

In this hut a drum was being beaten, which consisted of an earthenware vessel over which a wet goatskin had been drawn and allowed to dry. Two reeds were then taken and held over the drum in a milking position. With these the drum was beaten to produce a resounding boom. Other girls would rhythmically clap their hands and sing special songs. We started in the evening and kept it up until the next morning without sleeping; the older girls did not allow us to stop, as Nobathwa was also not allowed to sleep. We, who were of one age-group and many in numbers, had to watch over her. We sang lewd songs and used such obscene words that I, who am now a Christian, can no longer bring myself to use them. In retrospect I think with shame of all the sinful lewdness and realise that the king's days on this earth had to be numbered because he took great pleasure in lecherous obscenities.[77]

Nobathwa sat at the back of the hut behind a screen, and we all enjoyed what was going on. This was at a time when we still knew nothing about our heavenly father. Nobathwa was fed with meat. She was supplied with packets of sugar, coffee and salt and was always provided with a fresh supply of millet beer. Men were not allowed to enter this hut.

Z.104
G.137

The older, full-grown girls, those with fully developed breasts who were called *amakhikiza*, played the fool with us. We, who were of one age-group, were expected to retrieve glowing embers with our teeth from the open hearth. We younger girls protested, saying: 'Don't play the fool with us. The king never ordered that we should pick up burning coals with our teeth. The king himself can't do it!' We tried it once, but never again. The older girls, who wanted to lord it over us, tried to engage in fisticuffs and beat us. They then called on Nobathwa to do it. Some of our age-group then remonstrated with the older girls and said, 'You will be killed if Nobathwa suffers burns as a result of your insistence that she remove burning coals with her bare teeth.' Some of the *amakhikiza* then came to their senses and said, 'The girls are right.' They then desisted.

Z.105
G.138

While this argument was going on, I also approached the fire-place, but I did not take any coals. I said: 'You want me to get burnt, while I am still alive? I will rather allow myself to be beaten!' Some of the girls tried to pick up embers with their teeth but dropped them again very quickly. When Nobathwa approached the fire she was terribly frightened. The grown-up girls said: 'Pick one up! Come on, take it!' But she could not get herself to do it, but we all laughed when we saw how fat and corpulent she had become. We then said to the older girls: 'The glowing ember will stick to her fat and cause a bad burn. You will all be killed!' It was then that the older girls said: 'Indeed, you have prevented an accident. Guilt slips under the blanket without anyone knowing.'[78]

Z.106
G.139,
140
Every now and then woman messengers, sent by the king, came to enquire how big Nobathwa had grown. These messengers just looked into the hut and soon took their leave again. They never indicated that they had been sent by the king. On their return they reported everything to the king and told him how fat Nobathwa was. Rolls of fat had already formed under her chin, she had become so corpulent that she could no longer walk.

The time then came when we had to fetch wood and rushes for plaiting a special garment. The damp rushes had to be beaten till they were soft and white and woven into a covering. On the day she was led out of the hut Nobathwa was enveloped by this garment so that only her face showed. Her face was painted with red and white ochre. Zofazodwa Xulu functioned as Nobathwa's attendant. She was a girl as popular as Nobathwa herself.

Z.108-111
G.141
On the day on which Nobathwa was to leave the hut to be presented to the king, we all had to go to the river first to bathe. On the way back we again sang the obscene coming-out songs. We then paraded before the king who reposed on a seat, surrounded by his male attendants. He was amazed when he saw Nobathwa, saying: 'You have kept from me how fat Nobathwa really is. You always said she was just sleek, yet, now she looks like a mountain.' Nobathwa found it impossible even to perform a few dance steps. Her attendant danced on her behalf and, while we danced, she was allowed to sit down. The least movement caused her to perspire, and when she did, the perspiration ran off her body in rivulets. As evening approached, we were told to stop and ordered back into our huts on the grounds that Nobathwa was too tired. She was given millet

beer to drink to refresh her from the exertions of her stout-
ness, and thus she grew big faster and came out sooner than
her sisters, although she was younger than they.

Z.112
G.142,
143

On the day on which she left her hut two head of cattle
were slaughtered. One was given to the woman who had
brought her up. The second one was given to Nobathwa;
we of the same age-group shared the meat with her. After
we had eaten, we divested ourselves of the plaited cover-
ings made of rushes which we had been wearing. These
were burnt the following day, outside the *umuzi*.

The coming out ceremony of Nobathwa had been a
very elaborate affair; that of her sister, Usiyobi Nala, was
small by comparison because war with the British, which
led to the battle of Isandlwana, was threatening. The
ceremony was therefore shortened. Then followed my own
coming out and then that of Unozizwe Nala. In our cases
the celebrations were quite short and superficial because
the nation was already at war.

GIRLS OF THE *ISIGODLO* LEARN TO SHOOT

Z.114
G.144

We younger members of the *isigodlo* had great fun when
we were allowed to watch the older girls, the *amakhikiza*,
as they were being taught how to shoot with firearms. Girls
of the *isigodlo* who belonged to the age-groups making up
the Amadlundlu, Amaqwaki and Amaduku regiments were
instructed in the use of firearms. The guns with which the
king armed these young women were supplied by John
Dunn. The idea was that, while the army was in the field,
these young women would defend the royal residence, if
attacked by an enemy. How we laughed when we watched
them shoot. The king also watched, but he got very cross,
when, on firing, the girls threw the rifles down. We thought
this was a big joke and laughed heartily. But in due course
they learnt to shoot. John Dunn instructed them in loading
and firing. Thus these girls became the homeguard of the
king. He had greater confidence in them than in the men.

SNAKES APPEAR AT ONDINI

Z.115
G.145

Today I know that the Bible contains the truth. In the same way as Satan, in the shape of a snake, once deceived Adam and Eve, so have the Zulu people been deceived by snakes. Before the word of God and salvation through the Gospel became known, snakes visited the *imizi*; they were venerated as representing the spirits of the ancestors and animals were sacrificed to appease them. Since the advent of Christianity snakes do not visit our habitations as frequently as in the past.

I remember a startling experience at the royal *umuzi* of Ondini. I remember the arrival of four large snakes at Cetshwayo's residence. It was in winter and the harvest had not yet been completed when the first two snakes arrived. At first a large green snake appeared. It had a very long neck on which a dark spot could be seen. It was then said that a ravager had arrived, who must be Shaka. They said this because of the snake's wild and frenzied behaviour. On the same day on which the snake called 'Shaka' arrived, a second snake turned up, which was then called 'Dingane'. This snake was of a dirty dark-brown colour and was spotted. It was much bigger than the 'Shaka' snake. It was about as thick as a puff-adder, but very much longer.

Z.116
G.146

On the following day two more snakes came along, which were then called 'Mpande' and 'Senzangakhona'.[79] The one called 'Senzangakhona' was tawny-grey and much bigger than all the other snakes. It appeared to be very old and had poor eyesight and, for these reasons, it was also called 'Nyandezulu',[80] and regarded as the ancestor of all ancestors of the Zulu people. 'Mpande' was a young snake, about the same size as 'Shaka' and was of a light brown colour. These ancestral snakes were accompanied by many 'servant' snakes which made the hedge of dry branches their temporary abode. But, in addition, these snakes were also accompanied by a swarm of bees, which settled above the ancestors at the gateway. The snakes stayed in the hedge at the gateway; two on the eastern and two on the western side of the entrance. 'Shaka' and 'Dingane' were to the left, on the western side.

While the snakes were there no one was allowed to use that gateway. Cetshwayo ordered that a new entrance be opened and forbade the use of the gateway inhabited by the ancestors.

Z.120
G.147
The two snakes, which had arrived first, fought viciously with each other. They reared and struck at each other until they bled. We watched the fight. 'Shaka' seemed to be the stronger and on the way to defeating 'Dingane'.

The event of the two ancestors being bent on destroying each other was reported to Cetshwayo. He came to see for himself. The fight grew so furious, that Cetshwayo took fright, returned to his enclosure and disappeared into his hut. When he later returned and surreptitiously looked for them, they were still fighting. Standing on their tails they were intertwined and struck at each other. 'Shaka' over-topped his adversary by the length of his neck and bit with might. They were extremely angry and showed no fear of humans. They fought from early morning till late at night, bleeding extensively. Even 'Shaka's' green colour was tinged with red blood.

Z.123, 124
G.148
On the second day the *izangoma* [diviners] were con-sulted. They announced that 'Shaka' had come to kill Cetshwayo, but 'Dingane' was warding him off, so that Cetshwayo would not die; he was preventing it, that is why they were fighting each other.

When Cetshwayo heard this he became very angry and wanted 'Shaka' killed and burned. However, his attendants intervened, saying that he must not kill his father, for this snake belonged to the ancestral spirits. An ancestral spirit [*idlozi*][81] is not killed. The diviners also said that 'Senzangakhona' and 'Mpande' had come to make peace between the contending parties. Those two had not fought.

Z.125, 126
G.149
Cetshwayo's mothers also protested against the intended killing of 'Shaka'. His real mother, Ngqumbazi, born Zungu, was, of course, no longer alive; but he had staying with him one of Mpande's widows, Nomadada, daughter of Qopha Sibiya. Nomadada sent a message to the king's

grandmother, Langazane, born Sibiya, wife of Senzangakhona, who was living in her *umuzi*, Nokhenke, at Esixhibeni. She let Langazane know that Cetshwayo planned to kill 'Shaka'. Langazane sent the king a beast to calm him down and to persuade him not to kill 'Shaka'. This gift appeased Cetshwayo, who obeyed his grandmother, and desisted from his intentions. Not only was Langazane's beast sacrificed to appease the spirits of the ancestors, but Cetshwayo sacrificed many cattle of his own. I cannot remember how many oxen were slaughtered. He called on his paternal guardian spirits, Mpande, Dingane and Senzangakhona, and he thanked them for having saved him from death.

On the same day that the oxen were sacrificed sweet-smelling herbs were burnt in the sacred hut as an additional offering.

Z.129-131   The population showed due respect towards the ancestral
G.150   spirits, the *amadlozi*. The people covered themselves from head to toe and passed the snakes crouching low or even crawling past them on their knees, while calling out the royal salutation, '*Bhayede!*' After a short while the snakes disappeared. Their place of sojourn was sprinkled with the gall of the sacrificial beasts. A month later the king and his people resumed the use of this gateway.

Z.132-134   If this happened today, now that I am a Christian, I
G.151   would run away; I would turn my back on these things, and not even look, for I would know that Satan was operating through those snakes. Yet, at that time, I too venerated those snakes saluting them with the words, 'Royal Highness, *Bhayede*! Lord, Everlasting, you who command the lives of men!' This is how we venerated the ancestors, and we also praised them. All the people were greatly excited by all these happenings, the old people claiming that they had never experienced anything like this before.

ANCESTOR WORSHIP AND SACRIFICE

Z.135
G.152

The spirits of the ancestors were invoked by making animal sacrifices. This was done when people were plagued by sickness, or when the spirits appeared in the form of animals, or when a diviner, having thrown his bones, announced that 'those who are earth', or 'those from underneath', or 'those who appear in the form of animals', wish to eat.

Z.136, 137
G.153

Of the animals which the spirits of the departed use as temporary abodes, I have already mentioned snakes; but the monitor lizard[82] is also respected in this connection by some people. The Shabane and Buthelezi people, those who live in the Maphophoma River area,[83] paid homage also to the rock-rabbit [*imbila*]. The Shabane people furthermore do not eat small cattle.

Certain kinds of lizard [*intulo*] and tree-gecko [*isicashakazana*][84] were also revered. A male spirit is represented by a snake, a female spirit by an *intulo*. The name of the tree-gecko is a word to be respected as it is associated in the belief of the people with the spirit [*idlozi*] of an ancient queen. These animals were never killed if they were found at an *umuzi*. Before the advent of Christianity snakes frequently visited the *imizi*. They sojourned for two or three days and then departed. If a cat ever chanced to kill a snake it would be killed in turn. The snake was then buried in ash.

Z.138
G.154

On coming to the conclusion that the visitor represented the spirit of a departed headman or family head, word would immediately go out that beer had to be brewed. On that day the cattle would be brought home from their grazing at midday. Women and girls got dressed up in festive attire. An old man, with a worn skin blanket thrown over his shoulders, would enter the cattle-kraal. Looking towards the top end of the cattle-kraal he would single out the beast which was to be sacrificed. Deadly silence would ensue. The old man would then begin to recite the praise songs of the departed ancestors and to walk up to the sacrificial beast. He would then plunge his assegai into it, just behind the shoulder-blade, and immediately sit down. Again deadly silence would be observed.

The meat, food and beer, as also the assegai with which the sacrificial beast had been slaughtered were then usually taken to the main hut, but had to go round the back. One old woman was detailed to spend the night in this hut to watch over the sacrificial offerings. On the following day all the food was removed and consumed by the people.[85] After the meal clan songs were sung.

When the Buthelezi had made a sacrifice they sang:

> Wo, wa, wo!
> Wena wakwayiwa (liwa)
> Wayiwa amabele awoBaba
> Wo, wa, wo!
> Wayiwa amabele awoBaba!

> Wo, wa, wo!
> You who were once refused,
> Denied the corn of your fathers.
> Wo, wa, wo!
> You were denied the corn of your fathers!

The Dlamini sang as follows:

> Iphi indlovu eyahlula ezinye?
> Aph' amakhosi anezizwe?
> Wayiwa yè, wayiwa lè
> Mantongana lè
> Aph' amakhosi anezizwe?

> Where is the elephant which overcomes others?
> Where are kings who rule over nations?
> He was rejected here, he was rejected there,
> By the Mathonga far away.
> Where are the kings who rule over nations?

The national song of the Zulu is:

> Ha O Yi
> Ha O Ji![86]

CETSHWAYO ORDERS THE KILLING OF PEOPLE

Z.142
G.158
Gruesome were the occasions when the king caused people to be executed. There were many of them; but he was more considerate [than others], and did not have people killed without some reason or merely for the sake of killing. Masiphula on the other hand was quick in having people dispatched.

Z.143
G.159
Cetshwayo began with the *induna* of Ondini, Umkhokhwane, son of Nomo. First a hearing took place at which he was charged with having engaged in witchcraft. The executioners, called *izimpisi*,[87] bound him with leather thongs, dragged him to the rock of execution, kwaNkatha, and beat him to death with sticks.

Z.144
G.160
Soon after him Nyambose Magwaza was killed. He too was an *induna* at Ondini. He was being accused of having caused the death of people through witchcraft and the use of medicines. I watched as he too was bound with leather thongs, having been caught by a large body of men, beaten and driven to the rock of execution.

Z.145-147
G.161
Cetshwayo also killed Masiphula kaMamba Ntshangase, who had been King Mpande's chief councillor. Nobody laid hands on him, but he was killed through his drinking cup. Cetshwayo had confided to us girls that he had a grudge against Masiphula. At the time when the argument had raged as to who should succeed Mpande as king, Masiphula had used hard words about Cetshwayo, because he was in favour of Mbuyazi's succession. When Mbuyazi was killed in the civil war, Masiphula supported the cause of Mkhungo (a younger brother of Mbuyazi). He had maligned Cetshwayo and exclaimed, 'We shall never allow ourselves to be ruled by a fool!' He had a further grudge against Masiphula, because, as I have already mentioned, at the funeral of Mpande it was Masiphula who had disregarded Cetshwayo's directive, that a specific widow of Mpande, who belonged to the Mthethwa clan, was to be killed to accompany the dead king into his grave.

Z.154
G.161,
162
Cetshwayo hated Masiphula also on account of the fact that the councillor had found it possible to have his own son, Unozinkomo, killed because Mpande's daughters

loved him and he had made love to them. Masiphula was a strict guardian of Zulu custom and tradition. Cetshwayo was very fond of Unozinkomo and had interceded on his behalf. But as an unyielding custodian of Zulu custom Masiphula condemned his own son to death. I heard Cetshwayo say: 'If Masiphula was capable of killing his own son, who had committed no crime, he is capable of killing even me. He is savagely incompassionate.'

For these reasons he decided to do away with Masiphula. However, he dare not let his father's respected chief councillor die the death of a sorcerer or criminal by sending him to the Nkatha. He therefore decided to poison him secretly.

Z.146-150 Cetshwayo confided his plan to the girls who were re-
G.136,   sponsible for attending to the millet beer. These were the
164   girls Unkulunkulu Dube, Uqinisile Ngema and Qinisa Mngadi. Before the poisoning took place Uqinisile Ngema had let us into the secret, that medicine would be added to the beer. It was not long after this that Cetshwayo put his plan into action. I was a witness to the tragedy when Masiphula drank his doctored beer.

The position was that the two senior councillors, Umnyamana and Masiphula, kept their drinking vessels in the royal hut where each day they received a portion of beer from Cetshwayo. Each one had his own personal drinking vessel. One day at noon I noticed Masiphula perspiring excessively after having consumed his beer. We thought at first that this was due to his corpulence. But we then saw him get up suddenly to leave the royal hut. He greeted Cetshwayo, '*Sala, Ndabezitha!*' and added:'I have eaten and must now sleep. My whole body trembles and aches.',These were his last words. As he spoke his strength already began to leave him. We, who were sitting at the entrance greeted him, 'Farewell, father!'

At midnight it was reported that Masiphula had died. I soon learnt from Qinisa Mngadi, who was one of the girls in charge of the beer, that Cetshwayo had given her some *umuthi* [medicine], which he had received from John Dunn, and had ordered her to add it to Masiphula's beer. Cetshwayo said that only a little poison was needed as it would act rapidly. He himself had measured it.

Cetshwayo ordered that a reed mat be woven. Wrapped up in this mat the corpse was then taken to the deceased's *umuzi* at Mkhuze. Thus ended the life of this influential chief councillor.[88]

Z.155
G.165

The *isigodlo* girl, Umnondeni, and her father, Mantokwe Mtshali, were saved from a cruel death, because the king exercised leniency at the very last moment. She was in charge of one of the huts. Fire from the cooking place set a hut alight. When the king heard the roar of the flames in the proximity of his own hut, he asked excitedly: 'Who wants to burn me? Who lit the fire?' It was quickly reported to him that Umnondeni had started the fire. Almost beside himself with anger he ordered that she be taken immediately to 'the bewhiskered man' — the place of execution — and that her father should follow her. The executioners were summoned to take her and her father to the uNkatha. We were filled with great consternation and the king then enquired about the actual cause of the fire which had only destroyed a subsidiary hut. He was given the reply, 'Oh, King, the fire ran away and got out of the control of the girl!' The king immediately dispatched a fast runner who was to catch up with the condemned before they had been executed, countermand the orders for their killing, and bring them back. He succeeded and brought them back alive. The king's anger had subsided and turning to the girl he said: 'Child of Mantokwe, it is well that you are alive. I was angry, because my heart became alarmed, when I saw that my *umuzi* was burning.' He pardoned both the girl and her father; it was not alleged that he was a sorcerer. Mantokwe showed his gratitude by presenting a big ox to the king. However, the people were gossiping that his life had been saved because he was in fact a sorcerer.

Z.156
G.166

Another girl, Usimamayi, was condemned to death on account of a triviality. One of the king's beer ladles broke in her hand. She failed to report this to the king, who surmised that she was a witch who planned to kill him. He consulted the diviners who confirmed that the girl who had broken the ladle was an evil-doer. She was taken to the place of execution forthwith!

Z.157
G.167

On another occasion two girls, Unokufa and Zogile Khanyile, were killed because they had committed a crime. They had killed Shimayane, an elderly man, who, together with Johannes Ntuli, had been engaged to build the king's European-type house. The king had directed that these two girls should cook for the two workmen. One day Shimayane went to the cooking hut to enquire about his food. The two girls got cross, pushed him out of the hut and struck him with a knobkerrie and killed him. One of the king's man-servants, Mjunju Ngema, happened to come upon the scene at that moment and asked, 'What is going on here?' They replied, 'We are beating him because he insulted us.' Cetshwayo got very angry and challenged them, 'Are you the rulers of my residence as well?' When the sun had set they were no longer in the land of the living. All the people said that the two girls had killed themselves.

Z.158
G.168,
169

Living with us was also a young woman, Ungakanani, a daughter of one Makwaqaza, whose surname I have forgotten. She was surely engaged in some sort of witchcraft for she secretly managed to shave the hair off the head of one of the girls, Jabisa, the daughter of Tshingwayo. This happened on the following occasion. The king was indisposed and the whole 'inner circle' of his household had to be in attendance about his person. One group had to sleep inside the king's hut, the other group inside the *isigodlo* just outside his door. So it happened, that Ungakanani rose at night and shaved the hair off the head of Jabisa, while she was fast asleep. She did this because Jabisa was much beloved of the king.

When we got up in the morning and were busy putting our sleeping mats and blankets away, we saw what had happened, and asked Jabisa, 'Who has shaved your head?', but she did not know. We carried out a careful search and found the shorn hair in Ungakanani's bedding-roll. The shaving blade was also found. All this was speedily reported to the Chief Councillor who was 'father' to her; but not her real father. Mnyamane then said to the king, 'Ndabezitha, let her be judged by her own words; you have brought this matter before me as I am "father" to her.' The *izimpisi*

had to set her free. Mnyamana and the men then assembled
to interrogate Ungakanani. However, she admitted without
hesitation, 'I did it in order to kill her!' But the king then
insisted that the diviners should be consulted as well.
Ungakanani was removed from the assembly and the
diviners were admitted. The diviners declared: 'She is trying
to kill Jabisa, she wants her to die, because of the king's
love for her. She is also causing the king's illness.' When
she had been recalled, the king then said to Ungakanani:
'Alas, you are killing me, because you are staying with me.
I am sick, because you are killing me. What grounds have
you for complaint, do I not give you many presents? Have
I not made a cleansing sacrifice on your account, so that
you can stay with me? Why are you still dissatisfied?'

The king had undertaken these cleansing rites to enable
him to transfer this young woman from the *isigodlo* of his
late father to his own. He had taken her from his father's
isigodlo at Nodwengu. Cetshwayo wanted her to be near
him, because she was very intelligent.

The king then said to her: 'Go then, my child, the fault
does not lie with me. Enough, my child, you shall now be
married to "the bewhiskered man", uNkatha.'

The executioners took Ungakanani in great haste to
uNkatha, together with all the presents and gifts given to
her by both Mpande and Cetshwayo; they were so many
that they could have filled a wagon.

The remarkable thing is that Jabisa's hair never grew
again.

Z.159
G.170

Further, a girl from my own home country was killed.
She was Jikijiki, daughter of Sigodi Mnguni. She too came
from Mpande's *umuzi*, Nodwengu, and was established in
the inner *isigodlo* as one of the 'mothers'. She practised
trickery. Quite often she returned only after sunset. When
asked where she had tarried so long, she simply said that
she had gone to relieve herself. A few days later she indicated that she was not feeling well and had to leave the
umuzi for the purpose of an enema; but she disappeared,
because, in fact, she had fallen pregnant. This was reported
to the king. A search was instituted, but she could not be
found. All fords were guarded. Her clothes were taken to

the magic coil, the *inkatha*, to block her escape. Eventually, when her brother began to participate in the search, she was found; in fact, at not too great a distance from the *inkatha*. It was said that as she was under the spell of the *inkatha* she had been unable to move away and had been compelled to circle within a limited distance. On a certain day, when the sky was overcast, a small fire was spotted in an otherwise uninhabited area. The spot was surrounded and she was found, but not her lover. He managed to get away and made good his escape. To this day no one knows who he was or where he came from.

Z.160
G.171
When Jikijiki was brought before the king, he received her with a sneer, 'I greet you, Princess. I greet you, Princess of the Mnguni. Where, however, is our son-in-law?' But she remained completely silent. The king questioned her at length, but in vain. She did not betray her lover. At long last the king said: 'All right, we will see! I think you will talk when I have you married to "the bewhiskered man", uNkatha!'

Oh, the courage of this woman! I admired her. We all trembled with anxiety and felt as if we were going to die over this affair.

Z.161
G.172
Finally the king asked his chief councillor, Mnyamana, 'What shall I do?' He replied: 'I cannot answer, because she harmed you when she slipped out of your hands. Ndabezitha, do what you think right. You will not have killed her, for she has already pronounced her own death sentence.'

Turning to her the king thereupon said, 'I shall have you taken to "the bewhiskered man", uNkatha.' The men-servants quickly took her outside and handed her over to the *izimpisi*. The executioners then took her and all her belongings and led her away.

Z.162
G.173,
174
In conclusion I would like to mention that one of my own prominent relatives, Malambule, a son of King Sobhuza, was taken to uNkatha and killed. He had come to Nodwengu to greet King Mpande, when he was still alive, and paid his respects with a beast and 'its tail', that is, with two beasts. He was killed on account of his good looks. The king's councillors and servants made the king believe that

Malambule had come for the purpose of overshadowing
him with his own magnificent 'shadow'.[89] They said to the
king: 'Malambule has come to cast a spell over you with his
shadow. Do you not see how handsome he is? This *inkosi*
of the Swazis has a great shadow which will dominate you,
so that you will die and he will rule as king in your stead.'

When Malambule had set out on his homeward journey,
he was secretly intercepted and taken to the place of execution, kwaNkatha. He was the grandfather of *inkosikazi*
Alipha Dlamini,[90] the young wife [*umlobokazi*] of
Dinuzulu, who lived at Nobamba. She was the principal
inkosikazi of Nobamba.

Many more executions took place. I witnessed all the
incidents which I have described, except the last mentioned
one. On many a day we lived in great fear and anxiety.

MAKING RAIN

Z.163
G.175

In the year of the battle of Isandlwana I witnessed an
attempt by Dlephu Ndlovu at the royal residence, Ondini,
to make rain with the use of tar. When I think of it now I
cannot but laugh.

In that year there was a terrible drought. From the
Nkandla forest very long saplings were obtained. Their tips
were covered with black tar, which had arrived in a big drum
on one of John Dunn's wagons. These saplings were erected
on all huts, even those of the *isigodlo*. Before being erected
they were taken into the huts, as far as they would go, and
doctored with a few drops of gall from a slaughtered beast.
Word went round that it would soon rain. After a few days,
as no rain had fallen, they were taken down again and
soaked in one of the pools of the river. When they were
taken out again and brought back to the *umuzi* for re-
erection on the huts, one of the king's praise songs was
sung:

Behold the Silent-One.
Indeed, he doesn't quarrel with anyone.

But the sky was not even moved by this song and remained barren. The sun beat down mercilessly and scorched all growing crops. It was said that the ancestral spirits had declined [to assist]. On this occasion long, wooden pegs were driven deep into the floors of the huts to ward off any lightning and to stop it from entering the huts.

Later on, when I got to know what tar is I said to myself, 'Hawu, that lightning medicine was nothing but tar!' I then realised that this whole exercise had been nothing but deception.

MY NEPHEW MBILINI

Z.164
G.176-178

At the royal *umuzi* Ondini I also made the acquaintance of my notorious nephew, Mbilini, who subsequently became a freebooter and captain of brigands, thereby causing King Cetshwayo considerable embarrassment. He called me *babekazi*.[91] He spent three years at Ondini, while I was there. He gave the impression of being a kindly man, whereas in fact he was an hyena.

He too was a descendant of the royal house of the Swazi; he was a son of Mswazi. He tried to kill all his brothers; but he did not succeed, because some managed in good time to escape into a cave, into which Mbilini did not dare follow. Thus, for instance, his brother, Bunu, remained alive. In his *izibongo* [praises] he prides himself on the fact that he is:

> Imbokode kaHlubi
> Umaqothula yaqothula
> Abafowabo.

> The grinding stone of the Hlubi
> The relentless destroyer
> Of his brothers.

After that murderous attack he fell into disgrace with

his father and his people. When he was about to be killed, he escaped to Zululand and found refuge with King Mpande; but then Cetshwayo also said to him, 'Come to me, because your remaining brothers will want to kill you.' His youngest brother, Bunu, succeeded to the chieftainship, but died as a young man, of natural causes, after only a short reign.[92]

Z.165
G.179

Mbilini was a contemporary of the Ingobamakhosi regiment [1851 age-group]. He was still unmarried, but was already wearing a head-ring, because it was said that he was to be appointed as head of an *umuzi* and as such should appear as having entered a man's estate.[93] He was an intelligent man, of small stature and a dark complexion.

Z.166
G.180

Three years after his arrival at Ondini he left again in the company of two sons of Sihayo kaXongwa Ngobese of the Maqungebeni people. He betook himself to the Hlubi people, known as the abaQulusi. That was at the beginning of autumn [in the year] before the battle of Isandlwana. He first presented himself at the royal *umuzi* of Mnkabayi, a daughter of King Jama, and eldest sister of Senzangakhona.[94] He established himself in close proximity to her and built his own *umuzi*, which he called Indlabeyitubula. Here he made himself the *induna* of the abaQulusi.

Z.167
G.181

Accompanied by the two sons of Sihayo, Mbilini undertook numerous marauding expeditions. One of the sons was Tshekwane, who was eventually killed together with Mbilini; the name of the other one I have forgotten. They stole large numbers of cattle and sheep from the Boers across the Buffalo River. He contributed in no small measure to the outbreak of the war against the Zulus. These raids were like setting fire to dry grass which can no longer be extinguished.

Z.168
G.182

At first Cetshwayo did not appreciate that this would lead to war. Only when the whites rode in and recaptured their cattle by force of arms did he realise that a warlike situation was in the making. Later on, it was reported to him that Mbilini had even besieged white farmers; but they then pursued him and shot him dead. The report stated that he was riding towards his stronghold, Mbongweni mountain, which contained caves. He was riding with Tshekwane who was also shot. Cetshwayo became alarmed at the fact that he had also spilt the blood of white farmers and said dejectedly, 'Now Mbilini has started something.' So now Mbilini's bravado had come to an end. As I have said, he gave the impression of being a kindly man, but in reality he was an *impisi* — a hyena. If he had remained alive, he would have been quite capable of laying his hands on Cetshwayo himself.[95]

Z.169
G.183

I was still at Ondini when preparations for war were made. The British were kindling a war which Cetshwayo did not want. When he realised that the British were determined to make war, he set about mobilising [*phakela*] his own army. He assembled his regiments and ordered his medicine-men to 'doctor' them and treat them with protective and potent medicines. An ox, which had been doctored by the medicine-men, was killed. Without skinning it, it was cut up into strips. These strips of meat were thrown into the air and had to be caught by the soldiers, who sucked at them, spat out without swallowing, and passed the strips to the next men. After this ritual all the warriors had to take an emetic and then they were fortified by being sprinkled with protective medicines.

Z.42,170
G.184

The war began with the battle of Isandlwana.[96] As soon as Cetshwayo was apprised by his messengers that battle had been joined, he took his seat on the magic coil, the *inkatha*, holding the crescent-shaped *nhlendla* in his hand. He did this to ensure that his warriors would fight with unity of purpose, that they should not waver, and that victory would be theirs. It was generally believed that if the king was sitting on the *inkatha* the influence of his personality would reach out to his people ensuring the unity of the nation. His mothers urged him not to get up from the magic coil to go to the cattle-kraal. They maintained that if he did, the battle could not possibly end in his favour.

Fleet-footed messengers kept coming in with hurried reports about the progress of battle. When the king heard that his regiments were heading towards victory, he began to leave his seat on the *inkatha* every now and then.

But the mothers scolded him on that account. In the end it did not help much; the warriors returned from battle carrying the fury of war on their backs. They were covered in blood and had tied up their wounds with grass.

When it became known that a large Zulu force had failed to overwhelm the small British garrison at Rorke's Drift,[97] the mothers reproached Cetshwayo severely. They put the blame on the king for not having occupied the *inkatha* uninterruptedly.

THE KING'S FLIGHT

Z.171
G.185

I was at Ondini when the war drew to an end. It was then that British troops, coming up from the south, were marching on the royal *umuzi*. The king's older regiments became engaged with the enemy. But then one day, lights began to flash from the Emthonjaneni range.[98] Scouts were sent out and came back with the intelligence that the British had encamped themselves on the Emthonjaneni heights. On that day preparations were made for the king to flee. The *isigodlo* girls were ordered to collect all the king's personal belongings and to take them to a safe hiding place. We left on the very same day accompanied by two of the royal manservants, Lugede Sibiya and Mfezi Thwala. The one went in front of us, the other brought up the rear. We carried all the king's goods and chattels to Hlophekhulu and had to ascend the mountain, which is the home of hyenas and contains deep caves, to just below the white krantzes. With the aid of a rope the king's belongings were lowered into a deep cave.

Z.172
G.186,
187

We returned immediately and on the following day we carried our own possessions into hiding. On that day we consisted of a particularly large group; we were almost an army of our own. On our return we reported to the king that all goods were safely hidden. In reality, however, the king's possessions had been taken to safety for the benefit of those in charge; because when the king was captured and taken away, his possessions were retrieved by the men who had hidden them, and who enriched themselves thereby.

On that very same evening at sunset we left the royal *umuzi*, accompanied by the king, and marched to his late father's *umuzi*, Mlambongwenya. When we got there messages came in, indicating that the enemy had reached Ondini. We immediately continued our flight by moonlight and reached Landandlovu. We had come to the royal *umuzi* of kwaMbonambi late at night; but the intelligence that we were being pursued by British soldiers who were out to capture the king, forced us to flee further. The king went on foot and we walked with him. He hardly spoke a word.

Z.173
G.188

At daybreak Cetshwayo instructed his menservants to take all his wives, children and girls, as also all the cattle to Zibhebhu at Banganomo.[99] The cattle would serve our physical needs and ensure that the mothers and children would not die of starvation.

Z.174
G.189,
190

All that day we kept on walking, without sleep. From then on we no longer slept at any *imizi*, but under the open sky. On this journey it was my task to look after the [eleven-year-old] Crown Prince Dinuzulu. Then, at long last, we reached the place of the king's cousin, Zwide Zulu. It was at Zwide's *umuzi* that we had to part company with the king.

It was here that he selected twenty girls from among us who were to accompany and look after the children. In order that we might not be seen he ordered us to move only at night. I still remember how sore our feet became through walking among the thorns, especially at night when, without even a footpath to guide us, we could not see where we were going. The most gruelling part of our march came when we had to cross the waterless region of Bonjeni. No, my friends, we Zulus are really a tough people!

Z.175
G.191

At long last we arrived at Banganomo, the *umuzi* of Zibhebhu. Great was Zibhebhu's joy when he saw — not us, but the large herd of cattle following us. After our arrival we were split up. The women with children, and I, were taken to Enkalakuthaba. It was a small *umuzi*, but we were received with great kindness and well cared for. The *umuzi* was occupied by two women, who were both handicapped.

On the second day of our stay, Zibhebhu called on us and said: 'Now you will stay with me. In due course I shall restore you to your homes and people.'

But this he merely said to set our minds at rest, so that we would not run away. In reality, he had no intention of releasing us.

Z.176   A little later the two royal children, Crown Prince
G.192   Dinuzulu and Princess Beyisile, who were in our care, were removed by their uncle, Ndabuko, a younger brother of the king. He had his *umuzi* in our neighbourhood, still within the Mandlakazi area. But Zibhebhu refused to part with any of the cattle, which had been intended to provide the children with milk and meat. He made up a lying story to the effect that Cetshwayo had given the cattle to him as a present. He used them all for his own purposes and never made retribution for one single beast. He was a real Judas!

Z.177   As time went by it became known that King Cetshwayo
G.193   had been captured in the Ngome forest[100] and that the British had taken him away on board a ship. That meant the final end of the war. This was to Zibhebhu's advantage; because he could now keep the cattle without fear of further challenge. We also heard whispers that Zibhebhu now intended taking all the girls, women and children into his possession. All this persuaded us to flee; a decision which we put into effect three months later.

OUR FLIGHT FROM ZIBHEBHU

Z.178   In Zibhebhu's eyes we were already his property. He
G.194   had told his own people: 'Take care that they don't run away because I want to return them safely to their homes.' But this was a deception intended to allay our fears. Secretly he told his people not to make it known to us, that he would not allow us to leave. However, some of our relatives quietly told us about Zibhebhu's designs; because

he was also related by marriage to the Buthelezis. Zibhebhu was one of the Buthelezi sons-in-law. For instance, he was a brother-in-law of Saul Buthelezi, who later lived at the Esibongweni mission station, where he became a church-warden.

Z.179
G.195

In those days we also received visitors from our own people. These were Mashulane and Dladlule Buthelezi and Josiyase Dlamini. When they arrived one morning, they were hidden in the long grass nearby, because Zibhebhu was not to see them. They stayed in hiding for two days; we supplied them secretly with food. At the same time we prepared for our flight and found means and the opportunity for such an undertaking.

Z.180,
181
G.196,
197

At this time we were visited by one of the principal *izinduna*, who was related to me. When he saw me he said: 'Oh, this is where you are, daughter of my sister! Come, I will show you the way home.' His name was Mgwazi Mnyeni. I told him that I was not alone, but that there were quite a few of us from the same home area. We pretended being permanent residents of Zibhebhu's *umuzi* and had no further discussions with Mgwazi; because he was an important *induna*, and merely came to carry out inspections; but it became clear to us that he had an inkling of our intentions.

On the second evening we succeeded in smuggling our belongings unnoticed out of the *umuzi*; but we returned once again to fetch a few remaining possessions, and also to bid farewell to the crown prince, Dinuzulu, and his sister, Beyisile. Then we stealthily slipped out of the *umuzi* and never looked back.

There were the four older girls; Ziphezi remained behind; then of the younger girls there were four of us. Altogether four of our relatives remained behind. So the eight of us left the Mandlakazi, never to return. We reached Wele at sunrise and decided to rest and have a good sleep. Our travelling companions went to report our arrival to Ndabuko, a younger brother of the king. He invited us to come to his *umuzi*, where we received kind hospitality. We were regaled with meat, a mash consisting of mealies, sweet potatoes and pumpkin, called *isihhiya* [cf. *isijingi*], and beer. We noticed immediately that Ndabuko had made himself independent and was governing as a ruler. On the following day we took our leave, saying: 'Stay well, Ndabezitha. We must press on to reach home; but we shall call again.' He replied simply, 'Go then, and give my regards to your elders.'

Z.182
G.198

We continued our journey and eventually reached our homes where we relaxed and had a good rest. This was a most joyful reunion after a long separation. The festive atmosphere materialised a few days later when a big feast was arranged. Two big oxen and three goats were slaughtered. The first ox was presented as a sacrifice to the ancestors, who were thanked with the words, 'Spirits of our ancestors, we thank you for having safely brought back our children.' It was a delusion of our people, believing that the spirits of the ancestors would partake of the meat by coming at night to *khotha* [lick] it. What help can ancestors give us? I now wish our people would free themselves from these incomprehensible delusions!

OUR STAY AT HOME

Z.183
G.199

We spent a considerable period of time at home. As the rules of etiquette relating to the upbringing of girls were strictly applied we were held in tutelage and constantly instructed by the older, fully-grown girls — the *amaqhikiza*. A girl was not permitted to enter into a relationship with a young man without the approval of the older girls. After we had been instructed by them in the etiquette and rules of behaviour governing the association with young men, especially during the period of a betrothal, we were one day told by the senior girls to engage young men in conversation to encourage them in their approach to us. We immediately suggested, 'You talk to them; they can then approach us through you.' We suggested this because the young men had to secure the approval of our seniors in any case, before they could freely talk to us. Our seniors then enquired from us whom we particularly liked among the young men who approached them. They did this to be able either to encourage or to disillusion any particular suitor, as the case might be; and so we revealed to them who our favourites were.

Z.184
G.200

We had very many suitors. At times the young men arrived in whole groups; but the young men from our more immediate neighbourhood were not to our liking. Sixhwethu and I were enamoured of two young men of the abaQulusi clan, who lived quite far away. Our own people reproached us for falling in love with men from far away; but we replied: 'Our mothers belonged to the Ugudludonga [wall polishers] regiment; but we don't want to be wall polishers like our mothers, that is why our hearts wish to fly over the hills and far away!' This made our people laugh.

Z.185
G.201

We were in love with those two young men, and actually became betrothed to them. They both belonged to the Mazibuko family. Sixhwethu became engaged to Maweni and I to Shikashika. Some time after our betrothal the civil war[101] erupted. Hamu's[102] and Zibhebhu's people fought against the abaQulusi, who remained loyal to Cetshwayo. Our fiancés were both killed in the battle of Emhologo in Hamu's territory.[103]

Z.186
G.202

This civil war was later followed by another one which was fought because Zibhebhu had appropriated the king's cattle. During this time we lived in caves and suffered much hardship and many privations. We were molested by the people of Mandlakazi, Ngenetsheni and Mnyameni.

Z.187
G.203

However, before I tell more about our pitiful existence I should mention the underlying causes for the civil war. The hatred which caused the tension went back a long time. Hamu was really the originator of this hatred. On the occasion of the last First Fruits festival before the battle of Isandlwana, Hamu and Zibhebhu arrived for the festival with their followers armed with assegais. At Ondini they killed a number of Cetshwayo's people and even argued about stabbing some of the girls. One could smell the blood at the *umuzi*. The killings were started over a trivial matter. Hamu said: 'The young men who bring goods for the festival behave disrespectfully. They don't give way when I meet up with them.' This happened on the evening preceding the festival, when Cetshwayo was away from Ondini, having accompanied the amaWombe regiment to his late father's *umuzi*. Cetshwayo became very angry when he heard about this affair. Hamu left the *umuzi*, because he feared that Cetshwayo might kill him. It was from that day onwards that the relationship between Cetshwayo and the two confederates, Hamu and Zibhebhu, began to deteriorate. Later on, in their dealings with the British authorities, both Hamu and Zibhebhu kept on defaming the king.

Z.188
G.204

After the king's return from captivity,[104] we, who had been members of his former *isigodlo*, were invited to return to him. A number of girls from our *umuzi* went back to him. I too was on my way, but I only got as far as the *umuzi* of Mbatha at Inhlazatshe. There I fell seriously ill with severe chest pains and dreadful coughing. I was in tears when I was eventually compelled to wend my way home again; but this was my salvation. My enforced return home saved me from a dreadful calamity which later befell the royal *umuzi* of Ondini.

Z.189
G.205

Soon after Cetshwayo's return, the civil war, which I have already mentioned, broke out. It was started by Zibhebhu who was dissatisfied and annoyed because the king demanded from him the return of his cattle and his former *isigodlo* girls. Zibhebhu was a doughty warlord. Fighting broke out between his Mandlakazi and the royal Usuthu party. Zibhebhu took his opponents unawares. Cetshwayo was quite unsuspecting, when Zibhebhu suddenly appeared with an army and without warning attacked Ondini,[105] and many people and many *izinduna* and prominent persons were killed. Fortunately the royal children were not at home, but were visiting at the *umuzi* of Mankulumane; thus they were spared.

Z.190
G.206

The king succeeded in getting away, while the *umuzi* was already in flames. He managed to save himself, without being seen, because of the dense bush in the vicinity. However, while he tried to make good his escape, the king was accosted by a youth who wounded him in the side with an assegai. Cetshwayo called out, 'Mfana, you are stabbing me; yet I am your king!'

The king managed to reach Nkandla; but his wound caused him to become gravely ill. Here he was found by those who went in search of him, who said, 'Behold the king; he can go no further.' The king was so upset and deeply shocked by the fact that it had been a youth, who had assailed him, that this hastened his death. It is rumoured that the youth also died. Thus our king died lonely and deserted, and was buried at Nkandla. This is the information I received while I was at home.[106]

OUR STAY IN THE CAVES

Z.191
G.207

During the armed strife with Zibhebhu we took refuge among the rocks and krantzes and a cave in the mountain called Ngwibi. The whole mountain is called Ingwenya and the pass over the mountain is Isikhala sika Madlungulu. On this, the eastern side of the Ingwenya range is Mount Ngwibi. The cave is not near the summit but in a depression of the mountain.

This cave was discovered by Qina Buthelezi, while he was herding cattle in that area. He is the same man whom you, Baba Mhlahlela, baptised at Lemgo, when he received the name Zakarias. The cave was so big that even cattle could be accommodated inside at the bottom.

Z.192
G.208,
209

On the day on which we moved into the cave a white goat was sacrificed. The ancestral spirits were implored: 'Madlozi, you who belong to us, open the doorway, that we may enter, and that we, your children, may be saved. The enemy, who will kill us, if he finds us outside, is close at hand.' The goat's gall was sprinkled on the rocks and it was then said that the entrance had thereby been secured. The pouring out of the gall had truly opened the cave.

The men then entered the cave first, to see that everything was in order and safe; then they called out to us, 'Come inside! All is well and it is safe.' I was one of the last to enter. I was afraid that some of the huge boulders might come tumbling down on us.

By the friction of two sticks, called *uzwathi*, fire was made and all parts of the cave were lit up, enabling us to select nice dwelling-places within that large cave.

Penetrating the cave in the direction of the setting sun, we found deep inside a large pool of water. We turned back in a hurry when someone told us that this was the abode of a huge snake. This dark pool was quite frightening. It was fed by a spring, and its water emerged deep down in the valley. The smoke from the fires was dissipated through fissures in the rocks; they were such that no sunlight ever penetrated.

Z.193
G.210

The cave consisted of a series of large white halls. We found sleeping mats which were alleged to have belonged to Mzilikazi's people. It was said that these mats and the broken earthenware vessels, which we found, had been used by the juveniles from Mzilikazi's clan, who had occupied this cave during their circumcision ceremonies. An old woman who had been one of Mzilikazi's people and was still living in the vicinity, mentioned that it had been a custom, that should one of the circumcised boys die, the clay vessels which he had been using, would be broken where they stood. This woman also related that this mountain was inhabited by the Mzilikazi boys during their circumcision period. They were not permitted to have any contact with the occupants of the *imizi* in the vicinity. Those people who brought food for the circumcised boys never approached closely. They kept at a great distance and merely called out, 'Here is your food.' When one of the boys had died, their relatives were also advised by shouting: 'So-and-So is no longer in existence. He is dead.' The mourners were not allowed to cry, as long as there were still some boys whose wounds had not yet healed. Only when all had got well and could return home could the dead be lamented.

One day one of Hamu's and Zibhebhu's *izimpi* took up position at the cave, but did not find us, because we had withdrawn deep into the cave. Our enemies were afraid to enter. They sat on top of the rocks and called to us: 'Come out and show us where the cattle are; if you do as you are told, we will not harm you.' But we kept very quiet and stayed deep inside the cave, till they moved off again. Those with a little extra courage did venture to peep into the entrance of the cave; but they did not go inside. Our men, who were concealed near the mouth of the cave, would have immediately stabbed any entrant to death. So the enemy moved off again, without having even tried to enter.

Z.195
G.212
They also failed to get hold of the cattle, which were kept inside the cave. The cave was very large indeed. The cattle entered it from the west, and we from the east. The cattle suffered no hardship; there was sufficient grazing and water. The cows were not milked either to stop them lowing for their calves, when they were kept away.

Z.196
G.213
We, however, nearly perished from hunger; because we stayed there for nearly a year and were unable to till any fields or do any planting. We were reduced to searching for and digging up the tubers of a grass-like plant called *inkomfe* or *inongwe*. They resemble the *amadumbe*, but are much hairier.[107] We cooked them, but ate them without salt, because we had none. We also picked *inhlokoshiyane* berries. These berries we cooked and then ground them on stones, as we do with boiled mealie grains. We also searched the forests for edible tubers, such as the *izinongwe*, which are only eaten in time of famine; wild figs; and *izikhwali*,[108] tuberous veld plants, which we dug up. All these could be reached from our cave. I shudder to think of this famine! The Lord preserved us; but our suffering was great.

OUR JOURNEY TO HLIMBITHWA

Z.197
G.214
One day we spotted a wagon belonging to Shede Foloyi [Gert van Rooyen] on the road which skirted our mountain at that time. The wagon was loaded with sacks of mealies. We recognized him and ran down to him, that is, I, Diboli [Deborah], Meliyam [Miriam] and the mother of Andreas. We begged him to give us some mealies. For carrying we had a large *khamba*; this he filled for us. We then asked him if we could not travel with him. He was agreeable,

but said that he would return this way on the following day: 'I will meet you here again tomorrow; but bring your father and your mother as well.' He enquired if they were still alive, to which we replied in the affirmative.

Z.198
G.215
He then continued his journey with his wagon. People were greedy after mealies. He bartered thirty sacks of maize for forty head of cattle. On his return we six, that is, my father, Sikhunyane, his wife, okaMyeni, Diboli, Meliyam, Andreas and I accompanied him. Others, like Qina Buthelezi, remained behind. When Josia, who was staying with Hamu at Ngenetsheni, heard about this he followed and joined us later on. At the time when we ran away from Zibhebhu, Josia had remained with Hamu.

Z.199
G.216
On our way we had a frightening experience. We saw the body of a white man, who had been stabbed to death by Maphela, a son of Makhosana Zungu. We stood in the doorway and saw that his body had been covered up. Papers lay scattered throughout the house. We were told that it was the body of a missionary, the Reverend Schröder.[109] We were afraid of this place, fearing that the murderer might still be about and would want to kill us as well. I knew Maphele as he had attempted to court me and had followed me around. I did not love him; I already knew him as a murderer, as he had killed one of my friends, the girl Nomaqina Kunene. It was not that he had been courting her as well; but the lust to kill was just in his blood. In this regard he was just like my own kinsman, Mbilini. Nomaqina occasionally visited her relatives at Maphela's home, in the vicinity of the present town of Filidi [Vryheid]. He killed her not far from the home of the missionary whom he subsequently murdered. When he killed Nomaqina, she was in a party of four, two men and two women. He also shot Nonsukwane Sibiya, but he recovered. The bullet entered near Sibiya's navel and came out at his side. I knew that he was lusting after my own blood because I had rejected his advances. Maphele is still alive and lives on the Nkonjane. His father, Makhosana, accompanied Cetshwayo when he went overseas, and then returned. He was an upright person. During the war with Zibhebhu we were provided with

food by Makhosana, who treated us well.

Z.200
G.217 We travelled for six days and found the Buffalo River in spate. We stayed on the river bank to await the return of Foloyi [van Rooyen] who, in the meantime, had gone to visit his parents at Bivane. However, before he had returned, Kunesi Foloyi [Cornelius van Rooyen] had driven the wagon into the swollen river. The oxen lost their footing and began to drift. His brother-in-law helped to extricate them. They cut the riems[110] holding the oxen to allow them to swim to safety. The people were carried ashore and the wagon was pulled back. When Shede Foloyi [Gert van Rooyen] arrived he scolded them severely, because he had given orders not to attempt the crossing while the river was still in flood. We waited another three days and crossed after the water had subsided. In the meantime new riems had been cut and all the trek-gear put in order. We then continued our journey to Hlimbithwa which lies not far from Hermannsburg in Natal. It took us two days and two nights before we eventually reached Foloyi's home. Van Rooyen had us registered at Greytown; because everybody from Zululand, wishing to enter Natal, had to be registered. We were asked if we wished to be registered as belonging to van Rooyen's establishment. We all acknowledged that that was what we wished to be done; but father and mother were not registered because they were old. We then stayed with Shede Foloyi and lived inside his house. For my parents he built a hut just outside his yard. We then worked every day; but the work was light. During ploughing time we did the hoeing. Diboli was directed to work for his uncle, Welemu [Wilhelm].

2 Servant of God

I KNEEL BEFORE MY LORD JESUS CHRIST

Z.201
G.218-
220 Baba Mhlahlela, up to now I have related how, moving
on my knees and as a pagan woman, I served the king, day
in day out, for a long period of time. About the king's
nightlife with his *isigodlo* girls I must remain silent; because
as a Christian, who has now learnt to kneel before the
King of all Kings, the Lord Jesus Christ, I can no longer
speak about such things. I must now tell you how my
conversion came about.

For three years we stayed in the home of our master,
Shede Foloyi. In the third year I had a visitation by
the Lord, which then led to my conversion to Christianity.

My sister Meliyam and I used to sleep in the dining
room. One night, in a dream, a person [*umuntu*] came to
me. This person was shining-white [*mhlophe qwa*] like a
messenger [angel] and wore white robes. He said to me:
'Paulina, arise and accept this Bible. Go forth to where the
sun rises and teach my people, the old and the young!'
On top of the Bible lay a reader for young children and a
hymn book. After I had accepted these books, a tall,
dark person approached me and warned me: 'Don't take
this Book. If you open it you will surely die!' The messenger who had given me the Book then disappeared and I
awoke with fright. I then saw a huge flame of fire and
began to cry. I awakened Shede Foloyi, who got up
quickly and lit a lamp. I then told him what I had experienced that night. He then fetched a Bible and placed
it on the table. He then read to me from the Bible and
explained to me: 'You see, this messenger has been sent
by the Lord. It is the Lord himself who wants you to have
this Book. Jesus had revealed himself to you.' I replied,
'But I am not a Christian.' He smiled: 'The Lord will tell
you what he wants you to do. The Lord does not fab-
ricate lies.' These are the words which Shede Foloyi

addressed to me, he then added: 'Satan also appeared to you. It is he who wants you to reject this Book.' Van Rooyen then knelt down and prayed with me, and then got up and said: 'Go back to sleep, but call me, if you hear the Voice again.' We lay down again and slept peacefully throughout the night.

When I got up in the morning, I thought much about this vision, because I had not seen a Bible before and did not really know what it was. Shede Foloyi's wife had often told us stories about Jesus, also about Joseph who was sold into captivity; but I did not understand those stories. As a person who had come from Zululand I did not know anything of this kind.

Z.202
G.221 During the second night the gleaming white person appeared again, carrying the same book and said: 'Paulina, do not throw this Book away. With it you shall instruct my people where the sun rises, the old and the young.' He then continued to say, 'Do not be afraid when the dark person comes.' Then that other person did appear and threatened me, 'Do not open that book; otherwise you will die!'

Z.203
G.222 Again I awakened van Rooyen and said, 'The man carrying the Book has appeared again.' Van Rooyen said: 'He is not just a man, he is a messenger of the Lord. It is the Lord who wants you to take this Book.' I repeated what I had said before: 'But why? I am not a Christian. What shall I do?' Van Rooyen replied quietly: 'It is Jesus. He knows what he intends to do with you. Go to Him, for He is calling you. Fear not, but pray to the Lord. He will enlighten you.' He then knelt down and prayed and interceded for me, and read from the Bible late into the night. This matter weighed heavily on my mind and moved me deeply. Then, indeed I began to kneel before the Lord Jesus Christ and to turn to Him.

Z.204
G.223 This happened on a Monday. On the Wednesday Shede Foloyi saddled his horse and rode away to discuss this happening with the elders of the church. They then arranged for a meeting of thanksgiving at van Rooyen's house. On the following Wednesday they came together to hold a service and to bring thanks that the Lord had

manifested himself at van Rooyen's home. All those who had come gave thanks and praised God; these were his friends and relatives and the church elders. One Gert Botha, who was actually an elder of the Wesleyan church, preached in Zulu. I was called and had to stand in their midst. They said, 'We rejoice at the finding of this sheep, which once was lost.'

After the service I was questioned closely by Shede Foloyi who was also an elder. Eventually, in my perplexity, I asked again: 'What must I do? I am still not a Christian.' They said, 'Pray to the Lord!' But I remained perplexed and just did not know what to do.

I AM SENT TO THE REVEREND REIBELING

Z.205
G.224

Sometime later Shede Foloyi called on the missionary, the *umfundisi* Johannes Reibeling,[111] at Ehlanzeni, to acquaint him with these happenings. *Umfundisi* Reibeling — we called him Mangqashaza — thereupon arranged that one of his evangelists, Tobias Ngubane, should call at our place every Sunday to preach and conduct a service.

Umfundisi Mangqashaza directed furthermore, that I should be brought to him. There I was to attend school as a candidate for baptism. The *umfundisi* sent another girl who was to work in my place. When she came, I left and stayed in the home of the missionary. As I learnt very easily I was in three months ready to be baptised. Two important *abafundisi*, Haccius and Harms, arrived, engaged in a visitation of mission stations. A large gathering of missionaries [conference] took place at Ehlanzeni. On this occasion the church building at Ehlanzeni was consecrated.[112] On this same day I was baptised, in the company of four others, by the *umfundisi* Haccius. I was given the name by which the angel had addressed me: Paulina. I was overawed by the events of that day. The Reverend Reibeling told the two great *abafundisi* about my vision and *umfundisi* Harms took a photograph of me.

After my baptism a peace of mind came over me and I was filled with a new joy of life. *Umfundisi* Reibeling noted down a detailed record of my conversion. I stayed in his house a whole year, but left before the second year had run out.

MY ARRIVAL IN ZULULAND AS PREDICTED BY THE ANGEL

Z.206
G.225

I became a 'Kneeling-One' indeed, as unconsciously predicted by my father when he named me Nomguqo. I knelt down to accept Jesus Christ, the Lord of Lords; and having knelt down, the prediction of the angel, that I would go to where the sun rises, in order to instruct the people, both young and old, became a reality. After having stayed with the Reibeling family for over a year, Shede Foloyi, with whom I normally stayed, came to fetch me. At that time he was already living in Zululand which lay towards sunrise, to the east of us. He had acquired a farm there, after the war against Zibhebhu. We travelled by ox-wagon. We first trekked to Pietermaritzburg, and from there to Zululand. Eventually we reached the farm Melkboom in the Babanango district, where he had already completed his new house.[113]

Z.207
G.226

I began with the work of the Lord while staying with the van Rooyens. I kindled a fire in the hearts of the people; this spread and grew in intensity. I then saw for myself that the word of God is Truth. Yes, this fire from the word of God spread and set many a heart alight.

I first started with my own circle of family and friends. My half-brother and half-sister Andreas and Meliyam were the first to start learning; then from within my own family Diboli [Deborah] became a convert. I taught her in van Rooyen's home, and also conducted services at that place. Many people came to listen to the service, old and young, men and women.

Z.208
G.227-
229

So the weeks went by; then Satan used some persons as his tools and sent them along. They said: 'You are deceiving the people with the word of God. You are trying to get them into your power, then you and van Rooyen will take them away — overseas.' This notwithstanding, the older adherents remained firm. Among them were David Ntombela and Jesse Ntombela and Joseph Madide. They had become believers and read the Word of God; there was also a boy, Salomono Ntombela. Rebeka Ndima and a married woman, Jesaya Madide, adopted Christianity; so did a young girl Udleni Ntembu, who soon after died in the faith. Other converts were Ester Madide, Simon Ntombela, Magdalena Ntombela, the sister of Simon, who married Andreas Dlamini, and also Absalom and Ngwevu Khanyile. These were the first members of the congregation of Melkboom, which was later re-named Lemgo.[114]

The rumours and allegations that I was deceiving the people and that they would be sent overseas gradually came to an end as the congregation grew and became more firmly established. I shall mention this again later.

Through Shede Foloyi I sent word to *umfundisi* Reibeling that a congregation had been founded and that it was in need of an evangelist, as its numbers were increasing. I am happy to recall that the missionary replied very speedily. He sent Jeremia Buthelezi as an evangelist. When Jeremia arrived we already had quite a big, solid congregation at Melkboom.

The congregation became established in this way: both van Rooyen and I officiated as lay-preachers. On Saturdays Shede Foloyi and I discussed a theme for the sermon on Sunday. On Sunday we then both held a service. Foloyi preached to the Whites and I preached to the Blacks. We first started kindling the flame of God's salvation at his home, at Melkboom. Then we carried the torch to other places.

Z.209
G.230-
232

Our first call came from Badenhorst at Empembeni. The people warned me that Cas Badenhorst[115] would kill me with a bullet as he had a fierce temper. I simply replied: 'He will not shoot me, because he himself has called me. I am going in the name of the Lord.'

When he saw me come, he moved to meet me, '*Sakubona, Pawulina!*'[116] I returned his greeting; then I saw something incredible: he had his labourers working on a Sunday and had inspanned them like oxen to transport stones for building a wall. He held a whip which he laughingly applied every now and then in order to achieve a greater effort. When Shede Foloyi and I arrived, he called a halt and brought his labourers to the service. He, who behaved like a Pharaoh, attended our service as a modest and humble person; indeed, he turned out to be a good person. I remonstrated with him and showed him the error of his ways. He eventually admitted that it was wrong of him to carry on in this manner and he reformed. From then onwards he never again made his workers toil like animals. Until his death he tried to live like a Christian and he became a real Christian.

When the people realised what effect the word of God had had in converting a violent person into a reasonable human being, they stopped defaming me by saying that I was misleading them. They actually began to refer to me as *umPhositoli* [the Apostle].

After Jeremia Buthelezi had taken up his duties as evangelist, Cas Badenhorst also requested that he be sent an evangelist, who would teach at Empembeni. Elias Zungu was appointed; but he had to leave again, because, together with one Jakobina Zuma, he trespassed against the sixth commandment. He returned to Ehlanzeni and in his place Piet Zuma was sent to Empembeni. When I left Ehlanzeni, Jeremia Buthelezi, Elias Zungu and Mathewu Ngubane were still at the training-college [seminary] at Ehlanzeni. When they started working there, they also assisted in instructing those who had come to be taught by me.

At Empembeni I taught Stefa Ntombela, Piet Ntombela, Maria Ntombela, Ana Ntombela, Daniele Mabaso, Simon Zulu, Juda Mhlongo, Nathaniela Mdladla, Naftali Sithole. I went there every Sunday to teach and was usually accompanied by my half-brother and sister, Andreas and Meliyam, Lebeka [Rebecca] and Marta Zulu, and Josefa Madide; Susana also came along at times. I went with them in the mornings to preach, then we came back together and I preached again in the afternoons at home.

Z.211   We also went to Mandeva, which is now called

G.233   Esibongweni, and I preached on Thomas Joubert's farm, Vlakhoek. There another congregation was in the making. Jonathan and Saul Buthelezi and four Ntombela and Buthelezi girls were the first to become converted. Joubert had no evil habits; he too asked to be sent an evangelist. Mathewu Ngubane was made available. In the beginning his religious instructions went well; but then he sought the company of the men around the beer pots, he fell into the habit of taking part in drinking sessions on Sunday afternoons. The unity of the congregation fell apart when, on the occasion of a Christmas feast, he gave more and better food to the Ntombelas than to the Buthelezis. Partisanship developed, beer-drinks were held and the community life of the congregation broke up. Matters only began to improve again when Esibongweni was restarted from the beginning and Mathewu had been removed.[117]

Z.212   Branches of some congregations were started even
G.234   before Jeremia Buthelezi arrived. We went from place to place, preaching. During the initial period, for instance, we went to Babanango and preached in Andreas Liversage's house. Then we were called by a congregation which had formed at Manjekazi, beyond the Mhlathuze river. Then we broke fresh ground at Nansi Vermaak's. These different places for worshipping were visited in rotation. At Vermaak's a fervour was kindled, which led to so many conversions that, when a congregation had been formed, Vermaak asked for the service of an evangelist. But this congregation fell apart again when its appointed leader, the evangelist Mika Qwabe, became a renegade. He moved to Filiti [Vryheid] where he collected a congregation of his own, conducting services on Saturdays. The people then said, 'There is no real faith; the preacher has deserted.' However, even though he deserted, he had committed no sin. He was just headstrong. This had already been noticed at the training-school when the missionary once said, 'You've got as hard a head as all the Qwabes.' It is generally known that the Qwabes are a hard-headed people.

Z.213   The mission work at Emthonjaneni was started by
G.235   Mathewu Zulu. He became a convert at Empembeni and

was taught by Elias Zungu. Through his efforts a Christian community was established at Emthonjaneni; but when this had come about Benjamin Zulu was stationed there, followed eventually by Mathewu Ndlovu.

Z.214
G.236

The people who in the meantime had adopted the Christian faith through my own efforts were baptised by *umfundisi* Johannes Reibeling. He came twice; the first time on horseback, accompanied by his sons, Luwi and Welemu [Louis and Wilhelm]. He brought also with him some seminarists from the training-college, who could play brass instruments. Many people who heard the trumpets wished to convert to Christianity. The strange sound had pierced their souls. They said, they were facing destruction, because, surely, God had now arrived.

Z.215
G.237

Umfundisi Reibeling directed that we should all assemble at Melkboom as this was regarded as the centre of our work, because it was here that we had begun to proclaim the word of God.

A large multitude made up the congregation. I cannot remember how many were baptised. On that day everybody who believed in our Saviour came to Melkboom, many came from Mandeva and Empembeni; but the majority were from Mandeva.

Reverend Reibeling arranged that all matters concerning the congregation should be reported to Jeremia Buthelezi; he, in turn, had to keep me advised. A zealous religious life ensued. Jeremia preached mightily; the people loved to hear him, so did the Whites. He was a humble man, who placed his life at the service of the Lord. He was of a childlike, caring disposition. Kaas Batnos [Cas Badenhorst] presented him with a horse to assist him in his work.

Z.216
G.238

Two years passed by, then *umfundisi* Reibeling came for the second time; on this occasion, by oxwagon. He left the wagon at Vermaak's place and continued on foot. The seminarists again performed on their brass instruments, and again many were baptised on this day. He stayed a whole week to carry out a visitation of our mission field. His sons, Louis and Wilhelm, had again accompanied him and participated in the visitation. We first went to Mandeva (Esibongweni) and, on the second day, to Empembeni.

Those from the latter place were baptised at Melkboom, because they still had no chapel.

Z.217
G.239,
240

Thus the word of the Lord was fulfilled. I went east, in the direction of the rising sun, and here in Zululand and at Emakhosini, the heart of Zululand, I preached the Gospel. At the royal *umuzi*, Nobamba, two wives of King Dinuzulu[118] became Christians. One of them, Alipha Dlamini, who was related to me, I had instructed personally. Thus under the direction of Johannes Reibeling I taught the old and the young to accept the Saviour into their lives.

This was the beginning of my work in North Zululand under the Reverend Reibeling. This was called 'The Mission of Mangqashaza' [Reibeling]. I heard that Mangqashaza was doing mission work in this region quietly and unobtrusively, on his own responsibility, because the Hermannsburg Mission was at that time short of funds and could not afford to extend its missionary enterprise into this ancestral heartland of the Zulu people. Later on this problem was removed and matters came right.

Later on we were transferred to Ekuhlengeni and were ministered by *umfundisi* Volker. We attended Holy Communion at that mission station; also, those who had been converted were baptised there. At a later stage the Reverend D. Wolff took over this station.

Z.218
G.241

I never married although I received many proposals of marriage. I refused to marry, because I wished to dedicate my whole life to the service of the Lord and could achieve this best by remaining single. My brother was most anxious that I should marry, as I would have brought in enough *lobola* cattle[119] for his own marriage. Anyway, he did not lose out and actually got his cattle. Through my own toil I managed to acquire ten head of cattle, which I gave to him, so that he could not reproach me, if I remained single.

During the whole time when I preached and served the Lord, I remained in the employ of Shede Foloyi. He and his family treated me well and we understood one another. Even the attitude of his relatives towards me was good and kind.

WE ESCAPE THE HOLKRANS MASSACRE

Z.219,
220
G.242

Then came the war between the British and the Boers [1899]. As the eldest one I was to accompany Foloyi [van Rooyen] and his wife, who wished to move to Ladysmith.[120] But, on account of the fact that Ladysmith was in the process of being besieged by the Boers, we turned back; we therefore did not enter Ladysmith to make it our home. During the siege three of the family friends were killed: Nansi Vermaak, Badenhorst and one Welemu [Wilhelm]. However, we fled and made our way to my master's brother, Gunesi Foloyi, at Mthashana [Holkrans]. We remained there till the war had ended.

At that time a conflict with the abaQulusi arose. A number of Boers had congregated at Mthashana and were encamped in a wagon lager. It was rumoured that the abaQulusi planned to execute a bloodbath, but the Boers did not take these rumours seriously. However, the Lord preserved us from a fearful fate. Having heard what the Zulu servants were saying amongst themselves, I implored Shede Foloyi to leave immediately. I said to him: 'Please let us go home. A dreadful danger is threatening us. If we must die, it is better to die at home than in this place.' I had been warned by some of my own relatives who said: 'You will die with the white people; because you are living in their midst. They will all be killed.' At first I did not believe them, but in time I realised that an attack was being planned, and, in fact, that was so.

Z.221
G.243,
244

Chris van Rooyen, Shede Foloyi's son, who was an officer in the Boer army had not returned yet; but when I implored Shede, he offered no objections; he listened to me, because there was a good understanding between us. But the Boers in the lager treated their servants' talk with contempt. They said the abaQulusi were just 'poultry lice' and would be put in their place in next to no time.

But we packed up and left the lager, travelling day and night by ox-wagon. We trekked through *eNsubeni* [Langkloof] and, as we ascended the heights of Babanango and had reached the forest above Babanango, we were overtaken by some men who had just come from Mthashana

[Holkrans]. They told us that all the Boers at the lager had
been massacred. I was told by Jona Zwane that some
abaQulusi, who were in employment, had actually taken
leave to enable them to go home and to be 'doctored'
for war by their medicine-men, so that they could participate in this action.[121] The attack had been planned and
led by an abaQulusi chief, Sikhobobo Sibiya. He was a
short, spare man, just like Mbilini. Their hatred of the
Boers was great indeed. With tears I thanked God that he
had saved us from certain death. Jona Zwane said, 'You
can be grateful that you and your master's family have
been preserved.' Indeed, I was grateful, for the Lord had
saved us.

MORE WHITE MISSIONARIES ARRIVE

z.222
G.245
    Once the evangelical work among the Zulus had begun,
it grew and the need for another missionary, who would
lead and guide us, became apparent. The great shepherd
Jesus Christ sent us one of his faithful servants to take
care of us; he was *umfundisi* Bösser, accompanied by his
wife. We called him uBheseni. The beginnings were not
easy. At first he lived at Emthonjaneni on a portion of
land purchased on the farm Excelsior. In the year 1911
our mission then purchased a portion of the farm
Pandasgraf,[122] which adjoined Melkboom. *Umfundisi*
Bösser and his wife then moved from Emthonjaneni to
Pandasgraf and, under the most difficult circumstances,
they erected a church and a dwelling-house and called
this mission station Lemgo. My own family then established its own *umuzi* at this station. The missionary
also took care of the outstation. Two properties were
acquired. For the congregation at Empembeni he purchased
a site on which a house for the evangelist and a church and
school building could be built. At Emakhosini, the aban-
doned site of King Senzangakhona's original *umuzi*,
together with his spring, were purchased, so that the
people from the royal *umuzi* of Nobamba would have a

place to form a congregation.

Z.223
G.246

Umfundisi Bösser did not stay long in our midst. In 1922 our Heavenly Father suddenly called him away and he was buried in the graveyard of his mission station. Our congregation became orphaned, but *umfundisi* Junge, whom we called Fohloza, from the mission station Bethel, took care of us until we again had missionaries of our own. You, Baba Mhlahlela, came first; this was in October 1923. Three years later you were succeeded by *umfundisi* Uken; after him came *umfundisi* Johannes Peters.

During this period the Mission purchased Vlakhoek and established on it the 'jubilee station', Esibongweni, where both you and I spent some time in the service of the Lord. My main pursuit was the teaching of candidates and preparing them for baptism. When you left Esibongweni, I returned to Lemgo.

Z.224
G.247

I was overjoyed when at long last Masimba Buthelezi, who was in charge of the Nobamba royal *umuzi*, decided to heed the call of Christ and become a believer. After I had had a number of talks with him the word of God took root and he began to attend services, but shied away from baptism, because the mighty leaders of the Zulu people would not allow a Christian to be the commander of a royal *umuzi*. Eventually he resigned his high position in order to be free to become baptised.

I greatly rejoiced at the conversion of his kinsman, Ncitha Buthelezi, whom I had admonished and encouraged over a long period of time. You will remember that he was opposed even to the wishes of his wives to become Christians.

OUR COMMON EXPERIENCES AT LEMGO

Z.225
G.248

Baba Mfundisi, you have now heard my whole life history. I am grateful that you brought me here to Nazareth Mission Station, so that I could spend some time with you and you could note down my story. Many years have passed during which we have not seen one another, while you were here at Nazareth and I at Lemgo. I longed to visit you; now, [in 1939] my wish has been fulfilled. But the record of my story will not be complete if you do not include some of the events we experienced together at Lemgo. I am thinking, for instance, of the occasion when the king, Solomon,[123] came to Nobamba and denounced the practice of employing spirits in treating and healing people. A wave of mania and mass hysteria was sweeping the country and brought untold misery to the population, including members of our congregations. The people were tormented by a delirious illness of the brain, called *ufufunyane* and believed to be caused by evil spirits.[124] By the same token that Yehova builds His kingdom through the Holy Spirit, Satan has, as the innermost element of his realm, the spirit of deceit in which *ufufunyane* plays its part.

Z.226
G.249
What you found in this connection when you came to Lemgo did not exist at the time of the old Zulu kings. For this reason King Solomon requested the government to put a stop to the practices of medicine-men and witch-doctors who instilled the minds of the people with the *umoya wezwe*, the 'earth' or world spirit, and the *imimoya wezizwe*, the spirits of the people, of the *fufunyane*.

Z.227
G.250
You will no doubt remember Nafatali Sithole, a member of our congregation, who, with a horse and some additional money, actually 'purchased' twenty-four ghost warriors, young demons, and some *muthi* [medicine], with which he intended healing those who were obsessed by *ufufunyane*. This means he was aiming to heal those obsessed by *ufufunyane* demons by introducing other demons into them. He was using demons to exorcise demons!

Z.228
G.251
As far as I can see, this mental illness has come to us from the Thonga and Hlenga people. It also seems that Zulu men become infected with this obsession on the mines in Johannesburg and then bring it home with them. Before obsession by *ufufunyane* became known, people were possessed by *amandawu* and *amandiki*.[125] At the time of Bambatha[126] it was said that the people [rebels] were afflicted by *amandiki*. It was also said that the *ndiki* spirit came of its own accord or that it found access

to the brain through a person partaking of snuff. A person possessed by an *indiki* would be addressed as '*inkosi*', and anyone visiting such a person was expected to give him a small present. Again, if such a person had to diagnose the condition of another obsessed person, he or she would declare that the obsession was caused by the *amandawu* spirits, then that person would also be addressed as '*inkosi*'. These mediums diagnosed illness by throwing bones and always found that the illness was caused by the *fufunyane* spirits. This *fufunyane* sickness has been known in Zululand only as long ago as about the time when you first came here.

Z.229
G.252
The *fufunyane*, the ghosts of deceased persons, come mainly from those who were killed in battle, but not buried, and are split up into a number of regiments: there are '*izinsizwa*', '*isipoliyane*' and '*usuthu*';[127] *fufunyane* can come from any nation.

Ufufunyane can arise by itself or it can be brought about in a person by the action of medicine-men. When I enquired more closely as to how medicine-men get hold of *fufunyane* spirits, I was given a number of explanations. Some medicine-men place the network of fatty tissue surrounding the intestines on graves. When it becomes alive with maggots, they say the maggots are spirits, the essence of the corpses in the graves below. Others place open bottles containing fat on the graves, especially on the graves of evil persons. When the bottles are full of ants they are sealed and the ants are said to be the soul substances (*izithunzi*) of the deceased. Others again actually kill people and remove the fatty tissues. They rub the fat on their fingers and induce their patients, in whom they wish to implant *fufunyane*, to lick it off (*ukuncindisa*). Yes, there are also those who open graves to remove some bones, which they then use in conjunction with other magical medicines.

Z.230
G.253
I enquired further, 'How is this maniacal medicine applied to a person?' The bewitching process could be carried out by different ways and means; it depended on what one knew or had learnt about a person. One man, Mkhize, even maintained that one could obtain the soul

substance of living people and instil this into another person. For instance, a sorcerer only needs to collect some sweepings from a place where, say, a wedding party has performed, or from the front door of a church. These sweepings he will then mix with some of his own powerful medicines. Sweepings from a church were sometimes required because obsession of a Christian could be achieved only by using the *fufunyane* spirits of other Christians. The sorcerer then blows his whistle and calls out the names of the people whom he wants to become afflicted with the *fufunyane* sickness. The magic powder could be added to a person's food, or it could be strewn on a footpath used by certain people, or sprinkled in their yards or houses. This medicine does not lose its power, for whenever the sorcerer blows his whistle the spirits arise and become active. It then happens that the afflicted persons talk in strange tongues, emit deep and resounding sounds, and so forth. Afflicted Christians begin to sing like a congregation or preach like their *umfundisi*.

Z.231
G.254,
257

My enquiries about the nature of the *umoya wezwe*, the earth or world spirit elicited similar answers. Apparently it is invoked in similar ways. The sorcerer will, for instance, take used oil from a motor car and add it to his *muthi*. With this he will implant in a person the characteristics of a motor car. A person possessed by these demons will then imitate the movements and noises of a motor car. We observed this phenomenon in the case of one of our church elders, Hemeliyothi Ntenga, when he was treated with *fufunyane* while he had a haemorrhage of the lungs.

It was furthermore said that even a bull could become possessed by *ufufunyane*. A bull suffering from this sickness is likely to attack any person and to push him down a precipice.

We had endless problems endeavouring to combat these superstitions and evil practices in our congregations. Especially medicine-men who pretended or claimed to be converts but continued to treat their patients by having recourse to *ufufunyane* spirits caused us many a headache. Whenever we confronted them they started to argue violently.

Z.232
G.255

I still remember the embarrassing situation at Empembeni, when after divine service and in front of the whole congregation you called on Nafatali Sithole to account for his actions. Members of the congregation were afraid to speak up, but Sithole got angry and said he would lay a complaint against you with the government. But you got the better of him by telling him that King Solomon himself had asked the government to prohibit medicine-men from dabbling in *fufunyane* practices. The Holy Scriptures are also quite clear on this point, for in his letter to the Corinthians the Apostle Paul says: 'Ye cannot drink the cup of the Lord, and the cup of the devils: ye cannot be partakers of the Lord's table, and of the table of the devils' [1.Cor.,10.21]. And in his Gospel St Mark asks: 'How can Satan cast out Satan?' [Ch.3,23].

Sithole was subjected to church discipline, because the congregation had resolved that men who practised 'healing' through earth spirits and the spirits of the world and of people automatically excluded themselves from community with our Lord Jesus.

Z.233
G.256

More often than not, the people who profess to combat *fufunyane* by pagan practices, are the ones who actually spread this sickness of the brain. The reasons are obvious. If, for instance, a person is not well, let us assume he suffers from headache or a pain in the chest, and he consults a medicine-man who indulges in spirit practices, the medicine-man will readily diagnose obsession by *fufunyane* spirits, because an expensive treatment will bring in more money. He will not want to have purchased his ghost warriors in vain. The average price for one 'ghost warrior' is one beast. It is rumoured that some medicine-men possess large numbers of warriors, some even a large ghost population [*umphakathi*].[128]

A medicine-man might determine that a patient is being 'eaten up' (tormented) by an *indawu* spirit. He then suggests that *ofekezeli* [spirits][129] be implanted into the patient in order that they may guard the *indawu* spirit, preventing it from eating up the patient.[130]

In another instance it might be found that the patient is being 'eaten up' by *isipoliyana* spirits and that *izinsizwa* ghosts should be implanted to guard and protect the patient against the other sickness-spirits which possess him. These ghost warriors would be implanted into a patient not merely to protect him but also to wage war against and to destroy other spirits which possess him and are the cause of his mania.

Z.234
G.258

When the medicine-man has completed his diagnosis and the patient has indicated his willingness to submit himself to the suggested treatment the first step in the process will be the killing of a black goat. The medicine-man, with a show of great respect and deference will then say:

> Shwele Malangeni, Bhayede Nkosi!
> Ngiyashweleza nje, ngithi:
> Umusa nje, makhosi!

> I beg your pardon, Malangeni, hail nkosi!
> I just ask forgiveness and say:
> Graciousness only, *makhosi*![131]

At a ceremony at which the spirit of divination or the spirit of *ubundawu* is to be implanted into the patient, the following formula is used:

> Nansi imbuzi yenu, makhosi!
> Hambani kahle egazini lakhe,
> Nimsindise!

> Here is your goat, *makhosi*!
> Move pleasantly in his blood,
> And let him recover!

Z.235
G.259

The patient must then drink blood from the wound of the slaughtered goat and vomit it at the back of the hut. It would appear that when *fufunyane* spirits are being treated it is not unusual to lick fat of human origin.

After these proceedings water is stirred to a foam by using a number of medicinal herbs, such as *uhlungu-hlungu*, *umgwenya*, *ubububu*, *umadlozane* and others.[132]

While the water is being stirred to a foam for the treatment of *ufufunyane*, certain songs are intoned which indicate a revival of ancestor worship.

If the *indawu* spirit is involved the song would be:

Vuka Ndawu, kade ulele.
Nyokana hlazana mabone ubulawe!

Wake up, Ndawu, long time a-sleeping.
The little green snake might cause your sudden death!

Or:

Yo, yo, ho, ho, Ndawu,
Kuthi kazondi munti, Ndawu!
Nyokana eluhlazana,
Uma bonwa abulawe.

Yo, yo, ho, ho, Ndawu,
'Tis said, you hate no man, Ndawu!
Little green snake,
Whoever sees you, may he die.

Or:

Ayi, amaNthendelekwane.
Masal' oBonjeni.

Oh no, Nthendelekwane spirits.
They must stay on the Ubombo mountains.

Or:

Hamba Mfekezela!
Ufana nemamba.

Go away Mfekezela spirit!
You resemble a mamba.

In connection with the *izinsizwa* ghost warriors the following song is intoned:

Izinsizwa ezinkulu,
Ezaphuma oBonjeni
Lapha kungahambi khona muntu,
Umuntu efika afe kuleyondawo,
Akuhlalwa mpukane kuleyondawo.

The great *izinsizwa* ghosts,
They come from the Ubombo mountains
To where no human being goes,
Where any one who arrives will die,
A place where not even a fly will settle.

Z.236
G.260

The patient then has to undergo a cleansing by drinking some of the frothy water which acts as an emetic. Thereafter he must take some medicinal snuff. It is the same snuff medicine which is used when a person becomes a diviner. While he takes the snuff, the medicine-man implores the spirit, 'Nkosi, give wisdom to this person.' When he sneezes everybody present shouts 'Makhosi!' and a careful count is kept of the number of times he sneezes. As many ghost warriors as the times he has sneezed will take up their abode inside the patient. If he sneezed three times, three ghost warriors will be introduced. The function of these ghost warriors is to offer battle to the spirits by which the patient is possessed and which cause his sickness. The human heart thus becomes a field of battle for evil spirits.

Z.237
G.261

After this treatment the patient is cleansed through the sacrifices of a white goat. He must again submit himself to an emetic and some ablutions; then he must take some more snuff. The number of sneezes will now indicate to the medicine-man how many more ghost warriors must be implanted into the patient to act as guardians.[133] Once installed in a person, the ghost warriors remain for good. The snuff medicine used in this connection was previously used as a remedy for some affections of the gall-bladder; nowadays it is used as snuff remedy for people obsessed by *indawu*. It is prepared from the *ulusinga-lwesalukazi* plant.[134]

Z.238
G.262

The medicine-man will visit his patient from time to time in order to rouse the spirits by blowing his whistle. The patient falls into a trance and answers all the questions put to him by the medicine-man, without afterwards knowing what he has said. The spirits are then allowed to come to rest, the medicine-man blows his whistle to awaken the patient from his trance and tells him that the ghost warriors are keeping well and are ever watchful.

Z.239
G.263

One of our own church elders, Hemeliyothi Ntenga, an otherwise faithful soul, exemplified to us the falsehood and deception of these practices. When he suffered a haemorrhage of the lungs, his father called in a medicine-man, who treated him according to these practices. The haemorrhage was stopped; yes, even Satan can perform miracles. But from that time onwards Hemeliyothi stayed away from divine services. It is said that the cure of a medicine-man's patient is endangered if he attends at a place of prayer. However, we were not aware of what had taken place and one day we visited him and conducted divine service at the *umuzi* of his father, Palafini Ntenga. The text for the sermon was based on St Luke 19, 41–48 where Jesus weeps over Jerusalem. Even today Jesus sheds his tears over us, on account of our disbelief and because so many in the congregation tend to forsake Him again in order to follow the spirits of the world.

We had returned home again when a message was received from Hemeliyothi requesting the missionary to visit him. He had been struck by the message contained in the sermon and confessed his sin in having submitted himself to the indwelling of spirits. Having prayed for forgiveness he was granted absolution and Holy Communion.

Z.240
G.264,
265

But then it happened again. Hemeliyothi had another haemorrhage and in his anxiety, as the missionary was away at the time, he called in the same medicine-man. Again the bleeding subsided, but he found himself bereft of his senses. His wife called us and when we arrived we found him in a dreadful state. Goggle-eyed he was crawling around the floor imitating the movements and the sound of a motor-car. His wife begged us to pray and to beseech God not to let him die while of deranged mind.

We prayed and God did hear our prayer, for no sooner had we returned home when an urgent messenger begged us to come back again. On arrival at his home, accompanied by the missionary, we found that his mind had cleared again, but he was in a state of utter exhaustion. With tears streaming down his face he again confessed his sin and begged forgiveness so that he might die in peace. He received absolution and Holy Communion and soon after departed this life.

The case of Hemeliyothi Ntenga touched many a heart in the congregation and gave many something to think about, causing them to abstain or distance themselves from these evil practices.

Z.242
G.267,
269

Another matter which gave us many a headache and caused much dissension was that of polygamous marriages. I remember, for instance, Ben Sibisi who, after his conversion to Christianity, took a second wife and as a result came under church discipline. He withdrew from the congregation and lived the life of a renegade. But when I heard that he was gravely ill I reported this to the new *umfundisi* and related the circumstances of his apostasy.

The missionary visited Sibisi and, although received reluctantly, he was allowed to hold a brief prayer meeting. This fact aroused the ire of the churchwardens who called on the *umfundisi* as a body to complain and to warn him that he would cause a break up of the congregation if he visited apostates. They claimed people would now say, 'Let us continue to eat up all the "greens", and only when we see death approaching will we convert.'

Z.244,
245
G.270

Undaunted, the missionary drew on St Luke 15, 1—10 to explain how Jesus would go out to search for one lost sheep and rejoice when he found it; or the woman, resembling the Church, would search for one lost piece of silver and then cry out, 'Rejoice with me; for I have found that which I had lost.' While he was still expounding the Gospel, a young man rode up and said briefly: '*Umfundisi*, Sibisi needs you. He begs you to call on him.' Turning to the astonished wardens the *umfundisi* said, 'Now tell me what I must do.' Their answer was, 'There is nothing we can say but: "Go to him." ' They then took up their sticks and went home.

After confession and prayer Sibisi said that evil spirits were tormenting him and that he was longing for forgiveness and peace. He called his family together, including his second wife and, much to her consternation, he renounced his polygamous marriage. On the following day he passed away quietly and peacefully. The churchwardens never remonstrated again, when the *umfundisi* went in search of his lost sheep.

Z.246
G.271 Of the dates I like to remember, 27 August 1925 is one. On that day old man Dlamini was baptised. He was a typical old Zulu gentleman. He desired to learn about our Lord and Saviour and it became my task to instruct him. As he was keen and learnt diligently these lessons gave me great pleasure and I attended to them every day. Then suddenly he grew weak and his strength diminished visibly from day to day.

I asked the *umfundisi* to accompany me on my next visit. Dlamini wasted no time in voicing his request. '*Mfundisi*, show me the ford by which I may cross the wide river,' he said. 'I am old and sick and have not much longer to live.'

We both presumed that by saying this he wanted to convey that he wished to be baptised; but holding back a little, the *umfundisi* said, 'The river may be wide, but the ford is narrow.' Whereupon he replied, 'That may be so; but still, it is so wide that all mankind could pass through it.' Happily the missionary took him up on this: 'So you seem to know the ford already. You also know Jesus Christ, don't you, for Paulina has instructed you for some time.'

The old man shook his head: 'No, I don't know Him yet; show Him to me, that I may know Him.' We were somewhat perplexed and thought that he desired further instruction; but then he suddenly began to talk about the large and beautiful *umuzi* of faith with its central cattle-kraal: 'Big and small cattle, healthy and sick ones, old and young, are admitted to this cattle-kraal and are permitted to cross by the drift which leads to that wondrous *umuzi* of faith. Allow me to do the same, though I am just a bundle of bones.'

He was obviously in a state of great weakness, when the *umfundisi* said, 'But, Dlamini, did you not say that you do not know Christ?' 'Indeed', replied the old man with emphasis, 'and rightly so, because I can only really get to know Him, when I have been baptised in His name.' Having recovered from a fit of coughing he continued: 'As one inspans oxen, so God also harnesses people for His purposes. Let me also bear my yoke. If I were well, I would ask that you continue teaching me. But I am sick and will soon die. Please baptise me, that I may find salvation. I do know that He is the Saviour of sinners. Once I am baptised He will also become my Saviour.'

Z.247
G.272-
274
On our way back to the mission station, which was near by, to make the necessary preparations for baptism, we met Dlamini's daughter, who was still a heathen and had come from far away. Without prompting she said, after a brief exchange of greetings, 'Do complete the work you have begun with my father!'

Apparently she had dreamed that night that her father would be baptised on the following day. She had risen early to cover the long distance in time to be present at the christening ceremony. This astonished us; had we not decided only a few minutes ago to perform this rite! She must have inherited this clairvoyance and ability to dream of coming events from her father, who also had this ability. Dlamini once told me that some years ago, while at the coast, he had fallen seriously ill. In a dream he was approached by a beautifully garbed Christian of his own people who said: 'Dlamini, you are not ready yet to appear before God. Return home!' He never forgot this dream and it contributed largely to his later decision to adopt Christianity.

After baptism, at which he requested to be christened Abraham, his whole demeanour changed and it became obvious that he was now at peace with himself and the world, looking forward to enter the wonderful *umuzi* of his Heavenly Father. It was not long after this that he 'went home'.

Z.263
G.296
We Zulus have many customs [*imvelo*] which make it difficult for a Christian to decide whether they are objectionable heathen customs, or whether they are innocuous and compatible with life in a Christian congregation. In the beginning, for instance, we Christians did not attend the traditional funeral feasts [*idili*] at which the deceased are 'brought home'. Gradually this custom is being revived in our congregations. I am of the opinion that this is actually some form of ancestor worship, an occasion on which the ancestral spirit is made welcome to return to the *umuzi*. Piet Zuma never accepted invitations to attend such funeral feasts; but the evangelist Benjamin Zulu, and some of the churchwardens always accepted if they were invited to lead the devotions at which they would pray, 'God, collect the bones of the departed and bring them home!'

Z.264
G.297,
298
Earlier on I mentioned efforts to make rain by using tar and to protect Cetshwayo's *umuzi* against lightning. I laughed heartily when I later learnt what tar was, but I was appalled by this deception. It troubles me that some of our congregation still protect their dwellings by magic means, placing greater trust in the medicine-men than in Jesus Christ.

They call in a medicine-man, who collects some blood from incisions made in the heads of all inhabitants of the *umuzi*. This blood is mixed with *muthi* [medicinal charm] and with the fat of a black sheep, which has to be slaughtered on such an occasion. The medicine-man applies this ointment to sticks, called *abafana* [boys], which are stuck on top of the huts when a thunderstorm threatens. This treatment is believed to keep lightning away.

People also still believe that lightning can be attracted by the life essence of a person, which is contained in his blood. Again incisions are made in the heads of all inhabitants of the *umuzi* and blood drawn therefrom is mixed with medicine and smeared on smooth pebbles. These are then placed, preferably on higher ground, all around the *umuzi*. The lightning, which is invariably sent by a witchdoctor, will then not strike the people, but will be attracted by the blood on the pebbles and strike them.

Z.265
G.299
As I am old and my years are running out, I doubt whether I will live to see the abolition of these beliefs and customs which only lead people into darkness and distract their minds from the love and omnipotence of God.

Z.268
G.302
I give praise to our Lord Jesus Christ who has brought the Gospel of salvation to Zululand. In His name a congregation has been founded even at Emakhosini. I also give praise to the Lord who has led me safely throughout my life and who has allowed me finally to kneel before Him, to serve Him and to glorify His name.

Snapshots of Paulina in the Filter papers. The picture on the left is dated 1938; that on the right is undated.

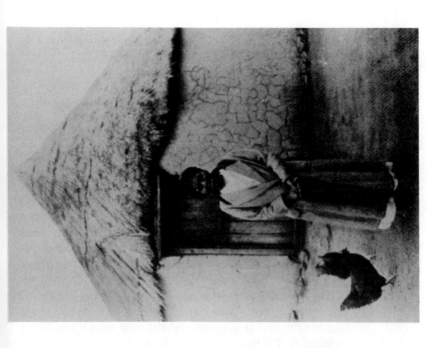

Epilogue

G.304
305 Paulina died on 12th December, 1942. She had been ailing
for about six months and was virtually bed-ridden for the
last three. Her strength was diminishing visibly but her mind
remained remarkably clear and until the last she dispensed
words of comfort, encouragement and advice to her many
visitors.

Mrs Sieglinde Peters wrote in a letter:

> At her funeral it became evident how well known and
> respected Paulina had been. Many heathens could be
> seen among the mourners. I stood with many Zulu
> women in the shade at the graveyard. We had gone
> there when the bell began to toll and when we saw
> the procession approach in the distance. The coffin,
> shrouded in black and covered with palm fronds was
> drawn on Paulina's own sleigh[135] by her own oxen —
> two white ones in front. In the absence of the resident
> missionary, Revd J. Peters, the funeral was conducted
> by Sibiya. All the evangelists, among them Elias
> Mkhwanazi, E. Mnguni and Jona Buthelezi, made
> brief speeches, most of them containing words of
> thanks; many male members of the congregation
> followed with a verse taken from the Bible.
>
> Next to her grave is that of Ncita, the father of
> Ephraim Buthelezi, whom Paulina had admonished
> over many years to become a follower of Christ. So
> she herself now lies buried in the graveyard at Lemgo
> amongst all those to whom during her life-time she
> had been a spiritual mother.

HEINRICH FILTER

To the Memory of

PAULINA NOMGUQO DLAMINI

Who Initiated The Congregations At Lemgo And Esibongweni

21. 12. 1887 — 12. 12. 1942

From Whoever Believes In Me, As The Scriptures Say, Streams
of Living Water Shall Flow Out From Within Him. John 7. 38

Notes

1 Mhlahlela. Revd Heinrich Filter's Zulu name, which means 'The one who settles'. Zulus like to give to white people with whom they are associated a name of their own, a nickname. This can be a corruption of the person's proper name or its Zulu form, such as 'Filiti' from Filter, or a name which refers to some physical or psychological characteristic or trait.

2 *isiGodlo* (pl. *iziGodlo*). 1. Upper part of the royal *umuzi*, reserved as the king's private enclosure, and consisting of the huts of the king's wives and children. 2. Women of the king's establishment; girls presented to the king as tribute or selected from the households of his subjects and, as his 'daughters', disposable by him in marriage.

3 Shede Foloyi. A corruption of the name Gert van Rooyen. In Zulu a person is spoken of or addressed either by his title or just by his name, not by a combination of the two. See also Note 1 above.

4 *umuZi* (pl. *imiZi*). Homestead, village; collection of huts under one head. Also: household, family; members of the family.

5 ubuThelezi (Buthelezi). One of the most prominent clans in Zululand. When Shaka subjugated all neighbouring clans and forged them into what eventually became the Zulu nation, the Buthelezi, being one of the most spirited and most warlike of the Nguni clans, resisted Shaka's efforts for many years, until they eventually fell victims to Shaka's superior strategy. But once they accepted the Zulu overlordship, they became one of the most loyal and reliable components of the Zulu nation. The Buthelezi chief, Nqengelele, was, in the words of the historian James Stuart, the 'great Shaka's guardian, adviser and friend'. His son, Mnyamana, was entrusted with the guardianship over Mpande's children. This Buthelezi chief served not only Dingane and Mpande, but became Cetshwayo's chief councillor and was the leading general in the Zulu army in the

Anglo-Zulu war of 1879. His great-grandson, chief Mangosuthu Gatsha Buthelezi became the first Chief Executive Officer of the Zulu Territorial Authority in 1970, and Chief Minister of the kwaZulu Legislative Assembly which subsequently followed.

6   Sobhuza.   Somhlolo, who has entered recorded history under the name of Sobhuza I, succeeded his father, Ndungunya, as head of a small chiefdom, situated between the Phongolo and Great Usuthu rivers west of the Ubombo range, about the year 1815. His chief wife was a daughter of Zwide, chief of the Ndwandwe, by whom he had a son and heir, Mswazi, who subsequently gave his name to the amaSwazi people. In addition to his principal *umuzi* at Shiselweni, Sobhuza had built himself another one nearer the Phongolo to which, strangely, he gave the name of kwaNobamba, which was that of a royal *umuzi* of the Zulu king.

7   Mpande, son of Senzangakhona, was a half-brother of Shaka and of Dingane. He succeeded the latter as king of the Zulu in 1840 and reigned until 1872, when he died a natural death. He was succeeded by his eldest son, Cetshwayo.

8   Piet Retief's grave.   Reverend Filter had heard on a number of occasions that Zulu men were joking about the fact that the re-mains of Piet Retief and many of his companions were not buried where the monument at Dingaan's Kraal stands, but that they were thrown into a donga nearby and covered by causing one of the banks to collapse over them. Encouraged by Paulina's statements, he took this matter up with various persons and organizations. As a result an examination *in loco* was carried out on 19 December 1956 by a group consisting of Professor C.J. Uys, Professor of History at the University of the Orange Free State, Mr Hennie van Rensburg, owner of the farm Uitzicht, where the donga was situated, Revd Filter, Dr P. Bloem and two other ministers of the Dutch Reformed Church, Revd P.P. Stander, superintendent of the Dutch Reformed mission station Dingaanstat, and one other missionary, and Mrs Kotie Roodt-Coetzee. The results were negative, but Professor Uys, the leader of the investigation, had a stone marker erected on the spot indicated by Paulina. The investigation was reported in some detail in *Die Volksblad* of 24 December 1956.

9   i(li)Hlaba regiment.   A regiment of Dingane, raised about 1837. *iHlaba* is also the name of the prickly aloe.

10   uNdlela [the Road].   He was appointed by Dingane, in succession to Mdlaka, to the position of commander-in-chief of the army and

senior *induna*, or prime minister, of the nation. He was the most important figure in Zululand after the king. He and an *induna* named Dambuza, also known as Nzobo, were the king's chief advisers. He is reputed to have strongly influenced Dingane in his decision to kill Piet Retief and his followers. Ndlela led the Zulu impi which ambushed and attacked a Boer commando at eThaleni. Dingane's army, led by Ndlela, was defeated on 30 January 1840, by Mpande, supported by the Voortrekkers. Thereupon Dingane had Ndlela executed by strangulation with an oxhide thong, and declared his body to be unworthy of burial.

11   Nhlanganiso was one of Dingane's master spies. He was better known under the name Mhlangana, but is not to be confused with Dingane's half-brother by the same name. Early in 1833 Nhlanganiso (Mhlangana), accompanied by fellow-spies, Mphezulu and Mgoduka, was sent into Ncaphayi's territory south of the Mzimkhulu to collect certain information about the Bhaca. When this information proved faulty Dingane ordered that the eyes which had seen what in fact did not exist should be plucked out, whereupon the three men were blinded.

12   Mhlahlandlela was, according to Paulina, one of the royal homesteads of King Sobhuza.

13   *Donga.*   Washed out ravine or gully, deep waterway. Adopted into South African English and Afrikaans from the Zulu word *u(lu)Donga* (pl. *izinDonga*), having the same meaning.

14   Historically established facts and also the investigation mentioned in Note 8 have rendered the Zulu version about the locality of Retief's grave untenable.

15   *inDuna* (pl. *izinDuna*).   Officer of state or army, appointed by the chief over others; captain, overseer; head-man, councillor.

16   Nomhlawathi means 'She, of the python'. The syllable 'no-' is prefixed to nouns to indicate a female, commonly in the names of women. *inHlwathi* (pl. *izinHlwathi*) is the Natal python.

17   This is an allusion to the so-called *lobola* custom whereby an essential element of a marriage agreement is the handing over of an agreed number of cattle on the part of the bridegroom's people to the father or guardian of the bride as compensation for losing her as a member of his family, and in order to ensure the right of the bridegroom to any issue of the marriage. In modern times *lobola* is often 'paid' in the form of money or some other goods.

18   When Paulina was still young only authentic, indigenous Zulu names

would have been in use. Growing contact with whites and conversion to Christianity led to the adoption of western, particularly biblical names, which were often Zulu-ized.

19 *isiCholo* (pl. *iziCholo*). The high head-dress, tuft or topknot, worn by married Zulu women. When her marriage is approaching a girl allows her hair to grow; then the hairs of the centre of the head are plaited with grass into a series of spikes which are then sewn together to form a truncated cone. This is then greased with a substance containing red ochre. The rest of the head is shaved. The *izicholo* which have the shape of an inverted basket are modern versions.

The reference to the battle of Ndondakusuka gives an indication of the time of Nomhlwathi's betrothal. The battle took place on 2 December 1856 between Cetshwayo and a rival faction led by a half-brother Mbuyazi (Mbulazi). Cetshwayo emerged completely victorious and thereby secured his eventual succession to the Zulu throne.

20 *inKosazana* (pl. *amaKhosazana*). Eldest daughter of the chief house in a family; daughter of a chief; term of respect for any unmarried lady.

21 *u(lu)Khamba* (pl. *izinKamba*). The general term for an earthenware pot or vessel. Different sizes and shapes, for special uses, often have specific names.

22 *umNumzana(e)* (pl. *abaNumzana(e)*). 1. Owner of an *umuzi*, village headman, family-head; 2. Gentleman, in modern usage the equivalent of Mister.

23 This early hour is picturesquely called in Zulu *mpondozankomo*, lit. 'the horns of the cattle'.

24 Ntabankulu (*iNtaba* mountain + *khulu* big, high). The 'high mountain', some 18 km east of Ulundi.

25 *isiVivane* (pl. *iziVivane*). Cairn, accumulated heap of stones, 'lucky heap' on which Zulus throw stones as they pass at crossroads or some outstanding place. The action is believed to bring good luck.

26 Duiker (Afrikaans origin). *Sylvicapra grimmia*, or any of several other small species of S. Afr. antelope of the genus *Cephalophus* sometimes called 'diving goat'. It is a brown or grey animal with small upright horns, and its height up to 60 cm, named duiker from its diving (*duik*) under the bushes when pursued.

27 *iNqomfi* (pl. *amaNqomfi*). Yellowthroated longclaw, *Macronyx croceus*.

28 Revd Schmidt had succeeded Revd W. Prigge at Emvujini mission

station and later succeeded Revd H. Müller at Endlangubo mission station.

29 In 1863 Revd H. Müller, accompanied by Revd Kück, had visited Prince Cetshwayo and had been invited by the prince to establish a mission station near his *umuzi*, kwaNdlangubo. This was done by the missionaries Müller, Fröhling and Kaiser. The station was called Endlangubo. The first dwelling built of reeds and thatch was soon destroyed by fire, in which the missionaries lost most of their possessions. A more substantial house was built in 1864 by missionaries Müller and Kück, assisted by two settlers, Knoop and Düvel.

30 The accepted way of crawling out of a bee-hive hut is head first, to make sure that no unexpected enemy or danger is lurking outside. By crawling out backwards Revd Müller gave the impression that he had less fear of possible dangers outside than of a treacherous attack from the inmates of the hut when he turned his back on them to crawl out in the accepted manner.

31 Such food would consist either of meat, mealies or *amadumbe* (see Note 66).

32 John Dunn, trader, hunter, and Zulu chief was born at Port Alfred in 1833, of English parents. His mother was Ann Biggar, second daughter of Alexander Harvey Biggar. He grew up at Sea View near Durban, but, losing his parents and his inheritance whilst in his teens, he took to transport riding and hunting, activities which eventually led him to settle in Zululand, where he became adviser to Cetshwayo and was given a chieftainship. He married young, his bride being Catherine Pierce (English father, Malay mother); but after he settled in Zululand he married an additional forty-eight Zulu wives. He died in 1895.

33 Two letters in the mission archives at Empangweni refer to King Mpande's death. One, dated 18 December 1872, written by Revd J.H. Kück at Endlovini states: 'Old Umpande has died. The royal princes have all assembled at Undini and have subjected themselves to Cetshwayo, so we do not have to fear the outbreak of war.' [Editor's translation]

The other one, dated 23 October 1872, written by Revd J.K. Rössler at Enyezane states: 'At long last it seems to be true, what was so often related as the truth, and yet was not true, namely that umPande has died. Yesterday all the important personages were ordered to make an immediate appearance before Cetshwayo to accompany him to uNodwengu, because his father was suffering great pain, etc. Only the important persons know a little. No one dares speak about this matter. But it is alleged (namely by the important persons, one of whom was very open towards me, and another one spoke frankly to Schmidt, because we were also *abakhulu* [important people]) that the prince wishes to keep umPande's death secret, until he has made his own preparations. A short while ago he ordered the demolition of all the smaller *imizi* and their amalgamation with the larger ones, in order to have better control and to thwart the witchdoctors — so he says; but now most people believe that this is a measure to stop people running away. It is possible, nay, probable that the old man has passed away. The concealment of this fact is facilitated by the custom that the body of a king, even if he dies at the beginning of a month, is not removed from his hut for burial before the new moon. There is so much tension and secretive specu-lation among the people, as I have not experienced before. Every day we expect a storm to break. The Lord preserve us!' [Editor's trans-lation]. Without indicating his source, Revd Filter added a note to the effect that Mpande died on 18 October 1872.

34 *umSuzwane* (pl. *imiSuzwane*).   Species of shrub, *Lippia asperifolia,* having a very disagreeable smell, used to suppress even more disagree-able smells. Used also for smearing the body as a protection against crocodiles and dogs.

35 In the case of sharp weapons, such as assegais, the blades were re-moved from the shafts and interred 'out of reach' of the deceased king, lest he got hold of them and caused his surviving dependants 'stabbing pains'. The burying of the blades was done with great secrecy.

36 The body-servant, *insila*, was in constant, close attendance upon his master. One important function was to receive upon his body the royal spittle, whenever the king wished to expectorate. This the *insila* would rub into his skin lest a witchdoctor got hold of some of it, as this was regarded as potent medicine.

37 On this occasion this consisted of some 1 500 warriors.

38 Emakhosini was the burial place of the ancient Zulu kings whose graves are scattered over a wide area. In a number of cases it has not been possible to identify and pin-point a particular grave, although the general locality of its site is known. Among the graves in this area or reputed to be, are those of Jama, Ndaba, Mageba, Punga, Zulu Nkosinkulu, Ntombela, Senzangakhona, and Dinuzulu.

39 Nobamba [the place of Unity and Strength] is by far the most im-

portant site of a royal *umuzi* in Zululand. Built by Jama it became the home of his son and successor, Senzangakhona, father of Shaka, Dingane, Mhlangana, and Mpande, and for this reason the best known of the early Zulu kings. See also Note 6.

40   The *inkatha* of the Zulu nation was the symbol of national unity and strength, and consisted of a grass coil a little less than one metre in diameter, the circular form of which was believed to have the power of collecting up all the traitors and disaffected subjects, and joining them together with the rest of the nation in affection for the king. It contained the *insila* or body-dirt of the king and his predecessors; also the scrapings from door posts and straw soiled by the action of their bodies passing in and out of the huts, their vomit, animal hair or teeth, and such other ingredients as might be prescribed by the *inyanga* or responsible medicine-man. The whole was shaped into a coil and wrapped in python skin, which in turn was securely bound with grass rope. An *inkatha* is handed down from generation to generation and the *inkatha* used by Shaka was kept right until Cethswayo's reign, when it was burnt by the British in the 1879 war. In addition to the Zulu national coil, personal *izinkatha* belonging to individual chiefs were in existence.

41   According to Zulu belief the spirits (souls) of the departed do not go to 'heaven', but rather underground, where they occupy the same social position as they did alive. The term *abaphansi* means 'the ones below' and refers collectively to ancestral spirits in a polite and euphemistic way.

42   Theophilus Shepstone (1817-1893) was Secretary for Native Affairs in the Natal Government. Somtsewu is a hybrid word, derived from the Xhosa-Zulu root *so* (father of) and *mtseu*, a Sesotho word meaning 'white'. Somtseu or Somtsewu therefore means 'white father' or 'father of the white man' i.e. a pioneer. See also Note 45.

43   Makheni was an old royal *umuzi* which had been built by Ndaba, used by his grandson Senzangakhona and rebuilt by Mpande. It was called Makheni [the Perfumery] because it was here that the king and the members of his household were periodically annointed with sweet-smelling herbs. Makheni stood on a ridge to the right of the Melmoth-Vryheid road, about six kilometres east of Dingaanstat. It was destroyed during the war of 1879.

44   Ondini (or more correctly oNdini) is the locative form of *u(lu)ndi* (sg. only) meaning 1. High pinnacle, apex. 2. Mountain range. 3. An alternative name of the Drakensberg Mountains. Applied to

this *umuzi* the name is an indication of its impenetrability. The original *umuzi* by this name stood not far south of Shaka's Bulawayo *umuzi* in the Eshowe district. After his succession to the Zulu throne Cetshwayo rebuilt Ondini on a rise east of Ulundi plain and three kilometres east-south-east from where the Ulundi battle monument stands today. It was burnt by the British after the battle of Ulundi on 4 July 1879. A portion of Ondini has recently been restored.

45 Shepstone and his entourage arrived at Mahlabathini on 25 August 1873. He was somewhat chagrined by the fact that the Zulu chief *induna*, Masiphula Ntshangase, had stolen his thunder, by proclaiming Cetshwayo King of the Zulus at Makheni a few days earlier and before he could be formally crowned by Shepstone himself. However, Theophilus Shepstone proceeded to crown him king at the Mlambongwenya royal *umuzi* on 1 September 1873 amid considerable pomp and circumstance. Shepstone paid a farewell visit to the king on 3 September and returned to Pietermaritzburg.

46 Cetshwayo wished his new *umuzi* Ondini to be an exact replica of Dingane's *umuzi* Umgungundlovu. Measurements made by the Revd R. Robertson, who was on friendly terms with Cetshwayo, give an indication of its size: it had a diameter of 747 yards (682 m), and an outer circumference of 2 354 yards (2,151 km). Between the inner and outer fences close on 1 000 huts were built in rows of three. The centrally situated cattle kraal [*isibaya*] was 90 acres (36,5 ha) in extent.

47 'Mothers' in the plural refers to the extended family system of the Zulus. In terms of this system, in a polygamous household, a child had as many 'mothers' as its father had wives. In everyday life no distinction was made between the natural mother and the acquired mothers, i.e. the father's other wives. Thus, in the case of Cetshwayo, all widows of his father Mpande he would regard as his 'mothers'.

48 The best description of the *isigodlo* area can be found in A. T. Bryant's *The Zulu People*, p. 473.

49 The Norwegian Mission Society under Bishop Schreuder founded, amongst others, a mission station at what is today known as Eshowe. Its first pastor was the Revd Ommund C. Oftebro. To the Zulu ear his first name sounded so much like *umOndi*, the name of a forest climber, whose aromatic bark and roots are used against flatulence, that the reverend gentleman became known by that name. His mission station consequently became known as kwaMondi (the place of Ommund).

50 The term *inKosi* (pl. *amaKhosi*) is the word for king, paramount chief, or chief; it is a term of respect for royalty or for a person in high governmental authority; lord, sir; also Lord (New Testament usage). The female term is *inKosikazi* (pl. *amaKhosikazi*) and is applied to the principal wife of a chief or headman; applied, by courtesy, to any one of the chief's wives, any lady, or married woman.

51 The expression *ukuba bagane indoda elihwanqa kwenkatha babesophile* (that they might marry the bewhiskered man at the Nkatha, after having bled) was a euphemistic term for condemning women to death and ordering their execution. kwaNkatha was the name of the place of execution of Ondini and must not be confused with the word '*inKatha*' for the sacred coil (see Note 39). According to C. T. Binns, *The Last Zulu King*, p. 56, the place of execution was some 'three miles distant from the royal *umuzi*, a flat bushy place opposite the uPathe hill, on the farther bank of the White Umfolozi River, situated about a mile or so below the uPathe drift.' The name kwaNkatha is presumably derived from the name of a person uNkatha, in the same way as kwaMatiwane, Dingane's place of execution at Umgungundlovu, was named after the prominent Ngwane chief Matiwane who died there. Apart from death by torture, the normal methods of execution were either by twisting the victim's neck, thereby breaking the spinal cord, or by strangulation, or by braining with a knob-kerrie. The reference to *babesophile* (after they have bled) is possibly an indication of execution by the last-mentioned method.

52 Archaeological excavations have revealed the foundations and floor of this particular house, as also window and door hinges, window stays, door locks, nails and screws. From the remains it would appear that the walls were built with sun-dried bricks, and that it had a thatched roof. In a diary, which he kept towards the end of the Anglo-Zulu war, Captain of Horse (Rittmeister) C. I. Müller, Baker's Horse, states under the date 5 July 1879 that at Ulundi: 'Cetshwayo had a rectangular house with glazed windows, wall-paper, door locks etc. A large mirror, as also a washstand were found in the King's house.' Müller went by reports he received from fellow-officers, because he himself was entrusted with camp duties at the Emthonjaneni, and did not participate in the actual battle of Ulundi (*Die Eiche*, Supplement No 22, 1957).

53 Among the Zulu observance of taboos [*ukuzila*] is closely related to the practice of *hlonipha*. To *hlonipha* means to show respect towards

a person either by acting in certain ways or refraining from certain actions, or by avoiding the use of certain names or words. The observance of taboos means basically that a person refrains from certain actions in relation to things, out of awe or the fear of unfavourable consequences. For instance a bride will *hlonipha* her father-in-law by not using his name; but people generally will observe the taboo [*ukuzila*] by never leaving a vessel containing milk uncovered during a storm, as the white milk is believed to attract lightning. There are innumerable *ukuzila* practices connected with milk and food, hunting, lightning, marriage, pregnancy, death, etc.

54   The ceremony of the First Fruits, held in December/January each year, was possibly the most important festival among the Zulus. It consisted of two parts, the Little *Umkhosi* and the Great *Umkhosi*. Until this ceremony had taken place and the king had given permission to do so, it was not permitted, on pain of death, for any one to partake of the new season's crops (especially green mealies). First Fruits ceremonies were not only held on a national scale, but also observed by individual tribes under their own chiefs.

55   *uLwezi* is the name of the lunar month which commences during October; so-called after the *ulwezi* insects which then appear. These are the grubs of the cicada which hide themselves in froth as they feed on the sap of young branches. *uZibandlela* (literal meaning: What pretends there is no road) is the fifth Zulu lunar month, commencing in November, when the paths are hidden by grass.

56   *u(lu)Selwa* (pl. *izinSelwa*) is the plant of gourd or calabash, *Langenaria vulgaris*. Its fruit, the *i(li)selwa*, (pl. *amaselwa*,) is eaten as a vegetable cooked as a marrow; the dry shells are used as containers for water or milk, ladles, etc. They are also turned into hand-rattles. They played an important role during the First Fruits ceremony.

57   In addition to the meaning given in Note 4 the word *umuzi*, (pl. *imizi*) is also the name of a species of fibrous plant, whose bark is used in making ropes, mats, and plaited sewing-fibre.

58   In the same way as the young men of the nation were grouped according to their age and then formed into regiments, so young women were gathered together in their own age-group regiments. When a male regiment received the king's permission to marry, an appropriate female regiment would be assigned to it, from whose ranks the men could then select their brides.

59   *Ndabezitha* is principally used when addressing royalty. It then means: Your Royal Highness; Your Majesty. But it is also used to

address chiefs or other highly placed persons.

60   Sorghum, panicle millet (previously called kafir corn), *Andropogon sorghum vulgare*, (*i(li)Bele*, pl. *amaBele*), was the basic grain used by the forebears of the Zulu before the introduction of maize into Africa. Sorghum is the basic ingredient of the traditional Zulu beer *utshwala*.

61   *Bhayede*, derived from *balethe*, means literally: Bring them, i.e. the enemy, for us to destroy. It is the Zulu royal salute: 'Hail your Majesty!', a term strictly applicable only to the reigning member of the Zulu royal house.

62   *iNgoma* (pl. *iziNgoma*). A dance-song performed at festivals, especially that of the First Fruits; royal song; national anthem; hymn, sacred song.

63   Mshelekwane (also Mtshelekwane) was the reigning chief of the abakwaMathenjwa, who occupied the central Ubombo area.

64   Catherine Pierce. See also Note 32.

65   Men with extraordinary gifts of speech and memory functioned as the royal 'praisers'. They made it their business to know everything that the king and all his ancestors ever did or ever had done, real or imaginary, and composed this mass of adulatory information in a series of terse phrases, in which metaphor abounded. These were recited, from memory, with machine-gun rapidity, in an almost never-ending sequence. An *imbongi*, in general terms, was thus a bard or professional praiser, who was attached to the court of every chief to proclaim publicly his praises (*izibongo*) or those of any notable visitor, ancestor or hero, on certain grand occasions or public festivals.

66   *i(li)Dumbe* (pl. *amaDumbe*). Species of plant of Arum lily family with edible tuber, *Colocasia antiquorum*, cultivated by the Zulus.

67   Ngayiyane. A chief of the Bushmen.

68   Revd H. Filter records Paulina as having stated: 'It is said that the Bushmen blind people with the rays of the sun. When the sun sets he is surrounded and attacked, broken into pieces and devoured by the Bushmen. Two Bushmen once visited Cetshwayo, they were reputed to have been medicine-men. When a big storm arose, people would say that the whirlwind was the dust of the dwarfs (Bushmen). The dwarfs would say: "You think you can see us! Where are we? Spot us, if you can!" If anyone were then to say: "I can see you!" the dwarfs would throw dust into his eyes.'

69   Zikhali was the son and heir of the Ngwane chief Matiwane. He

married Nomlalazi, a daughter of the Swazi king, Sobhuza I, and settled in the upper Thukela area where he tried to rebuild his broken chiefdom.

70 Paulina stated that at this point Cetshwayo became angry. He realised that he was the target of the satire, because he presumably knew that the people at the *umuzi* called him behind his back *usixoshwa 'kudla*, the food-chaser.

71 He does this because he is stingy.

72 It is almost impossible to translate this verse literally into intelligible English. This translation gives the meaning in the most general terms.

73 Paulina stated that when this verse was recited Cetshwayo must have realised that his brother Dabulamanzi had composed this song because only he called his brother 'Ishalashala'.

74 When a person approaches, the crocodile immediately disappears into the water; when the food arrives Cetshwayo knows nobody.

75 *Imiphand' ibhulawa yizakhelani*, Zulu proverb. A type of large earthen pot is known by the name *umphanda*. Neighbours are in the habit of borrowing them, and are the people most likely to break them. Furthermore, it is the neighbours who know where these pots are kept, and if they want to be vindictive, they can easily break them. Thus, it is one's friends from whom worst harm may be expected, or, literally, 'Pots are broken by neighbours'.

76 Meaning, when he has nothing to eat, he is sociable (laughs with others), but when food is put before him he has no time for anyone else.

77 Paulina's retrospective embarrassment reflects the attitude of her time. The primness of the Victorian age and the rather strict adherence to missionary principles made little or no allowance for the customs and practices of people still living very close to nature. At that time conversion to Christianity even demanded a change from traditional Zulu to European dress. In our more enlightened era a reversal of this trend has set in and greater tolerance is shown. Nowadays even ordained Christian Zulu ministers may be found who, on special national occasions, will shed their priestly garb and wear traditional Zulu dress. Zulu customs are likewise evaluated with greater leniency and understanding. There is a growing appreciation that, notwithstanding their superstitious, magical and profane features, many customs served a useful cultural purpose, especially if such customs were part of the traditional preparation

of young people for the rôle and position they would have to fill in
family, social and community life.

78 Zulu proverb: *Icala lembul' ingubo lingene*, meaning: Trouble
raises a blanket and comes in, i.e., somehow, trouble never can
be kept out.

79 Snakes played an important rôle in the ancestor worship of the
Zulus. They did not believe in a reincarnation of the departed in
the form of snakes but rather that snakes belonging to certain
species were a means of communication between the spirits and
those living on earth, or were personifications of the spirits of more
recently departed ancestors. In the occurrence described here, the
four snakes were identified with Cetshwayo's three predecessors and
their common father, Cetshwayo's own grandfather, Senzangakhona.
I have not been able to find corroboration of the snake's visit and
fighting from any other source. Having regard to Paulina's proven
veracity in many other instances, her account, amazing as it is,
should not be dismissed as a pure flight of her imagination. Further
research might yet cast more light on it.

80 *iNyandezulu* (pl. *iziNyandezulu*). Normally this refers to a species
of green snake, with black markings about the neck and sides.

81 *i(i)Dlozi* (pl. *amaDlozi*). 1. Human spirit or soul. 2. Departed
spirit (so called before it has gained entrance into the body of the
amathongo, ancestral spirits, by the *ukubuyisa* [bringing back]
ceremony). 3. Guardian spirit.

82 The monitor lizard is more commonly known as leguaan, likkewaan,
iguana; species of *Varanus*, usually *V. niloticus*, the water iguana
(leguaan). The Zulu name is *uXamu* (pl. *oXamu*).

83 This is in the vicinity of the Esibongweni mission station.

84 The *iNtulo* (pl. *iziNtulo*) species of lizard, salamander, *bloukop
koggelmander*, and the *isiCashakazana* (pl. *iziCashakazana*), play
an important rôle in folk-lore and are generally disliked by the Zulu.
The latter, a species of small salamander or tree gecko, is surreptitiously regarded as the *idlozi* (Note 81) of an old woman, and
carefully avoided lest it should be harmed with evil result. The
former conveyed to the people on earth the message that eventually
they would have to die. The real villain in this legend is, of course,
u(lu)nwabu, the chameleon. *Unkulunkulu*, the Great-great One,
sent *unwabu* to the people on earth promising them eternal life.
Then *unkulunkulu* changed his mind and sent the fast *intulo* to
overtake the chameleon, if he could, and command that people

should die after all. However, if the chameleon had already delivered its promise, it should be allowed to stand. The *intulo* raced off and had no difficulty in delivering its warrant of death, because *unwabu*, naturally slow, had furthermore tarried at a *khwebezana* bush (*Lantana salvifolia*) to taste the luscious mauve berries, of which it was particularly fond. The one had failed to deliver the good news in time to prevent the other from conveying the bad news, so both are disliked to this day for what their forebears did at the beginning of time.

85 Sacrificial offerings, for example, meat and beer, were never burnt or destroyed. They were set aside, overnight in a hut. The spirits were believed to come and merely lick at [*kotha*] the offerings, which thus remained undiminished in volume, and were subsequently consumed by the people themselves.

86 With reference to the Zulu national song, P.W. Wanger writes in his *Konversations-Grammatik der Zulu-Sprache*, 'In Zulu poetry it is unique, as it consists of interjections only. King Ndaba was the originator both of words and tune. When, as a growing boy he tended the herds of his royal father, Punga, assisted by his brothers, and playfully building cattle kraals with little stones, as boys will do, he accompanied his activities with the following song. In the evenings the valleys would resound with this strange song, never heard before, as Ndaba and his brothers drove the cattle home; and thus with word and melody Ndaba won a throne. Punga appoints him as his successor, and Ndaba's song becomes the ceremonial song on festive occasions. Senzangakhona raises it to the status of the national hymn, which, on pain of death, may only be sung on sacrificial occasions and during the first-fruits ceremony.' [p.653, Editor's translation] The words are as follows:

> Ha ô ji iji ji ji ô
> Awôye yiya woyé ya ô
> U yéyé iya ô

87 *iMpisi* (pl. *iziMpisi*) has the following meanings in normal use: 1. Spotted hyena. 2. Very ugly, vicious-looking person. There are also other meanings. It was a weird sense of humour which caused the executioners to be nicknamed hyena-men!

88 In one of his notes Revd Filter states that Masiphula made life very difficult for the missionaries. He was opposed to the Christianization of the Zulu people, as he feared that this would undermine and

eventually destroy the customs, traditions, and the very identity of the Zulu nation.

89 The word 'shadow' [*isithunzi*] denotes in Zulu, inter alia, a person's soul or personality. The shadow is connected with the spirit in the Zulu mind, for they say the shadow is that which will ultimately become the *ithongo* or spirit when the body dies.

90 Revd Filter sought some information from the *inkosikazi*, Alipha, about her grandfather, Malambule. She advised him through the agency of an evangelist, A. Nkosi, that her grandfather had come to Zululand to serve under Cetshwayo. In time, gossip would have it that Malambule had participated in the murder of Dingane. As a result of this Cetshwayo feared that the alleged murderer planned to 'overshadow' him with his own personality [*isithunzi*]. He therefore resolved to have Malambule killed.

91 *uBabekazi* (pl. *oBabekazi*).   My father's sister, my paternal aunt.

92 Concerning Mbilini, Revd Filter has left a note in which he states: 'I requested Pastor A. Mhlongo to obtain some information about Mbilini from old Jacob Mkwanazi and to advise me in writing. The report which I received states: "Mbilini's father was Mswazi and his mother was Nomkhasiso, born Vilakazi. He was born in Swaziland at Mswazi's royal *umuzi* called Hoho. There he was brought up by his parents, who did not wish him to be brought up like all other boys, learning to perform ordinary tasks and duties. He was to learn nothing but the art of war. They taught him to perform many evil deeds. When he was about twelve years old a dog was caught and skinned alive in the presence of the boy. The fresh skin was pulled over the boy's head and left there till it had dried out, the object being, to transfer the vicious nature of the dog to the boy. Then a man was bound hand and foot; the boy was given an assegai and told to stab the man until he was dead. This he did without hesitation. Innumerable similar atrocious deeds formed part of Mbilini's training." '

93 Every Zulu man of mature age (say, over forty years old) carried on his head an *isicoco* [head-ring] as a permanent fixture. It was assumed only after a specific order from the king or chief to some particular regiment of appropriate age. It was a formal and public recognition that now these men had attained their majority, as men. It conferred upon them a new dignity and superior status. More prized than the decoration itself, however, was the privilege which accompanied it, namely, that of marriage.

94 Mnkabayi, a woman of strong personality, had exercised considerable influence on the history of the Zulu nation, throughout her long life. Shaka had had some regard for his maiden aunt when he took over his father's throne, because she had been kind to his mother Nandi. But this did not stop Mnkabayi from conspiring with her other two nephews, Dingane and Mhlangana, to do away with Shaka, when she thought that his excesses had got out of control. During successive reigns she held the position of *induna* in respect of a number of *amakhanda* [military kraals].

95 One of the conditions which the Natal Government had included in the ultimatum presented to Cetshwayo's emissaries on 11 December 1878, was that Mbilini, and some others, were to be surrendered for trial by the Transvaal courts. Cetshwayo would have agreed to this, but had no opportunity of doing so.

96 The battle of Isandlwana took place on 22 January 1879. The British camp was annihilated.

97 Following the battle of Isandlwana and during the evening and night of 22–23 January 1879 a portion of the Zulu army launched a heavy attack on the British garrison at Rorke's Drift, but was repulsed with huge losses.

98 The flashing lights emanated from the British heliograph signalling apparatus. Emthonjaneni [loc. at the spring] got its name from the fact that here was situated the spring from which Dingane obtained water for his exclusive personal use, whilst residing at Umgungundlovu.

99 Zibhebhu kaMaphitha was chief of the Mandlakazi. He was a member of the Zulu royal house for his grandfather Sojiyisa and Cetshwayo's grandfather Senzangakhona had been brothers. Zibhebhu was an outstanding military leader, who had served his king well, as *induna* of Gqikazi, and during the Anglo-Zulu war. He was one of the thirteen kinglets appointed by Sir Garnet Wolseley at the conclusion of the war, but on the restoration of Cetshwayo rose in opposition to him.

100 The capture was effected by Major Marter with a squadron of Dragoon Guards on 28 August 1879.

101 The 'civil war' following the Anglo-Zulu war, was waged, on the one side, by certain dissident factions led by Zibhebhu, and, on the other, the royalists, loyal to the cause of Cetshwayo and his heirs.

102 Hamu was a half-brother of Cetshwayo, but of uncertain loyalty. At the battle of Ndondakusuka (see Note 19) he had supported

Cetshwayo; during the Anglo-Zulu war he placed himself under the protection of the British; after the war he made common cause with Zibhebhu against the royal house.

103 Revd Filter gives the date of this battle as 2 January 1881; but the editor has failed to identify this battle and to confirm the date.

104 Cetshwayo was put ashore at Port Durnford on 10 January 1883, and again installed by Sir Theophilus Shepstone on 29 January.

105 On the morning of 21 July 1883.

106 In this instance Paulina merely repeated what she had heard. The facts of the case are, however, that Cetshwayo had fled to the Nkandla forest and seems to have recovered from his assegai wounds. On 15 October 1883, he moved to his new Gqikazi *umuzi* at Eshowe. Its former locality is indicated by a memorial stone near the present police station. On 8 February 1884, the king died suddenly and unexpectedly. A senior medical officer was called. As he suspected death by poisoning he suggested a post mortem examination. This was, however, refused by the king's family, as it would have entailed cutting the body. The refusal was so vehement that the doctor feared that grave trouble might result, should he pursue the matter further. He certified death as due to 'syncope, the result of disease of the heart', in subsequent literature usually referred to as 'fatty degeneration of the heart'. The true cause will never be known. He was subsequently buried near the Nkandla forest.

107 The *inKomfe* is described as a species of tuberous plants of the *Hypoxis* sp., also yielding good fibre for ropes; and the *iNongwe* as a small herb whose tubers are used in time of famine, *Hypoxis* spp. For *amadumbe* see Note 66.

108 The *inHlokoshiyane* (pl. *izinHlokoshiyane*) is a collective name for small trees of several species of *Rhus*, some with edible berries. The name *isiKhwali* (pl. *iziKhwali*) refers to species of tuberous veld plants, e.g. *Vigna triloba, V. vexillata, V. glabra.*

109 According to the *Missionsblatt* of November 1883 missionary Heinrich Schröder was murdered by one Maphela on 6 June 1883. See *Natalia* 14, 1984.

110 A *riem* is a thong of softened raw hide used for numerous purposes instead of rope.

111 *umFundisi* (pl. *abaFundisi*).   Missionary; minister of the Gospel; title of Reverend.

112 The Revds Haccius and Harms were directors of the Hermannsburg Mission. The consecration of the church at Ehlanzeni took place

on 21 December 1887.

113 The acquisition of farms in Zululand by white farmers had become possible because Boer volunteers who had assisted the heir to the Zulu throne, Dinuzulu, in his fight against Zibhebhu, were rewarded with grants of land.

114 So named after the ancient town of Lemgo in North Germany.

115 To the Zulu ear and tongue 'Cas (Caspar) Badenhorst' became 'uKaas Batnos'.

116 '*Sakubona*' [I see you] is the normal Zulu greeting. The Zulu spelling of the name Paulina, is 'Pawulina'.

117 Paulina explained further: 'We began with services in Van Rooyen's house, then we went to Vlakhoek (Mandeva) now called Esibongweni, then to Empembeni. First came the Evangelist Jeremia Buthelezi; followed by Mathewu Ngubane and Elias Zungu. The fourth one was Micha Qwabe.'

118 Dinuzulu was Cetshwayo's son and heir.

119 For *lobola* see Note 17.

120 Paulina refers to Ladysmith by its Zulu name *Mnambithi*, so named after the Mnambithi river [Klip River] on which it is situated. The river's name means 'The Tasty One', as its water was considered to be particularly palatable.

121 Holkrans is the name of a farm, about 33km from Vryheid on the road to Zungwini and beyond, where a commando of 56 Boers was suddenly attacked by a body of Zulus on the night of 6 May 1902; most of them were killed. A monument marks the site.

122 The name *Pandasgraf* has no connection with Mpande's grave. The farm by this name is easily 25km or more from Ulundi. It is on the Ulundi plain that Mpande had his royal *umuzi* Nodwengu and that is where his grave may be found. The reason why *Pandasgraf* was so named is not known.

123 Dinuzulu died in 1913 and was succeeded by his son Solomon. The reason why Solomon denounced the practice of employing spirits in treating and healing people may emerge from the following circumstances. Isaiah Shembe, Zulu prophet and founder of the *Amanazaretha* (Church of Nazareth), was born in 1870 and died in 1935. Because of Shembe's great reputation as a healer and leader of men he acquired an ever-increasing influence over Zulu chiefs wherever he went. As he went about Natal, preaching, driving out demons, guided by the Holy Spirit, he also waged a spiritual war against the *izangoma* who were introducing spirits into people

and/or driving them out by other spirits. One might assume that in the process he brought an influence to bear in this direction on Solomon, because, eager to stress his relations with the royal house, Shembe gave Solomon one of his daughters, Zondi, in marriage. He also built a special house for him at Ekuphakameni, the headquarters of the church. There is a hymn in Shembe's hymnbook referring to Solomon's relations with the church.

124 *u(lu)Fufunyana(e)* (sg. only) is broadly defined as a disease, which causes delirium and insanity; a type of brain disease; mania; hysteria. These conditions are recognised by medical science as mental afflictions which are classified under the term *culture specific syndrome*. Disorders under this term are found amongst different people in different parts of the world under different local names. *Fufunyane* is thus peculiar to Zulus, under special circumstances in specific areas. It is recognised as a mental condition which requires treatment, and prescriptions for treatment — mainly of a psychiatric nature — have been evolved.

125 The origin and meaning of *amaNdawu* is obscure. These spirits seem to be connected, however, with the amaNdawu people who were skilled magicians. Doke & Vilakazi define *i(li)Ndiki* (pl. *amaNdiki*) as a person suffering from an hysterical disease (as known among the Thonga people); person possessed. Bryant defines *i(li)Ndiki* as: Person (mostly girls) suffering from some neurotic or hysterical disease (perhaps St Vitus's Dance) prevalent in the north of Zululand.

126 Bambatha Zondi was the reputed leader of the 1906 Zulu unrest.

127 The following meanings attach to these nicknames: *izinsizwa*, vigorous young men approaching manhood; *isipoliyane*, type of brain disease; *usuthu*, royal house.

128 The normal meaning of the word *umphakathi* is: an assembly of the men of a district; commoners, the common people. It is applied here figuratively to a ghost population which has taken up its abode inside a person.

129 *oFekezeli*. The ones that 'go wavering up and down'.

130 The belief in the efficacy of any magical substance or medicine, when implanted in a person's body, especially by means of incisions in the skin, is very strong. The purpose would be to strengthen the body and to imbue the person with properties he did not previously possess, or to protect him against and to ward off sickness and all evil influences. This possibly also explains why injections of whatever kind are normally very popular with Zulu patients.

131 Makhosi. In this context an appellation in addressing or saluting the spirits of the departed.

132 *u(lu)Hlunguhlungu*: A species of peppery shrub, *Vernonia corimbosa*; root used for doctoring calves, for stomach trouble, and to procure abortion. *umGwenya*: A species of forest tree, kafir plum, *Harpephyllum caffrum*. *uBububu*: A species of climbing plant, *Helinus ovata*, used as an emetic and as a love charm; Zulu soap plant. *uMadlozane*: A species of small syringa tree. *Turraea floribunda*: The roots were used to create a neurotic state for witchdoctor's dancing.

133 This is obviously good business for the medicine-man, for
1 sneeze = 1 ghost warrior
1 ghost warrior = 1 beast.
Therefore: 1 beast per sneeze!

134 *u(lu)singa-lwesalukazi* [lit. old woman's sinew]. Certain species of plants with tough fibre, e.g., *Asclepias physocarpa*.

135 Sleigh, sledge, *slee*: Ox-drawn, V-shaped wooden runners with crossbars or platform, for the conveyance of goods.

Select Bibliography

Works consulted in translating and editing.

Binns, C. T., *The last Zulu king: the life and death of Cetshwayo*. London, Longman's, 1963.

Branford, Jean, *A dictionary of South African English*. Cape Town, O.U.P., 1978.

Bryant, A. T., *A Zulu-English dictionary* . . . Mariannhill, Mission Press, 1905.

Döhne, J. L., *A Zulu-Kafir dictionary* . . . Cape Town, Pike's, 1857.

Doke, C. M. and Vilakazi, B. W., *Zulu-English dictionary*. Johannesburg, Witwatersrand University Press, 1972.

Krige, E., *The social system of the Zulus* (3rd impression). Pietermaritzburg, Shuter and Shooter, 1965.

Lugg, H. C., *Historic Natal and Zululand*. Pietermaritzburg, Shuter and Shooter, 1949.

Muret, E. and Sanders, D., *Encyclopaedic English-German and German-English dictionary* (4 vols). Berlin, Langenscheidt, 1897 and 1900.

Samuelson, R. C. A., *The King Cetshwayo Zulu dictionary*. Durban, Commercial Printing, 1923.

Shorter Oxford English dictionary on historical principals . . . (2 vols). Oxford, Clarendon Press, Repr. 1965.

Wanger, P. W., *Konversations-Grammatik der Zulu-Sprache*. Mariannhill, St. Thomas Aquins Druckerei, 1917.

Index

Zulus who converted to Christianity and adopted Christian names are entered under their clan names; e.g. Buthelezi, Jeremia; Dlamini, Paulina Nomguqo.